THE END OF MAN

Austin Farrer

THE END OF MAN

HODDER AND STOUGHTON
LONDON · SYDNEY · AUCKLAND · TORONTO

CONTENTS

EDITOR'S PREFACE

A careful survey of Austin Farrer's literary remains had disclosed few sermons besides those compiled in *A Celebration of Faith* which together with his earlier collection *Said or Sung* (published during his lifetime) constituted a significant legacy in its own right. However, in Katherine Farrer's attic-loft, where the beams meet the floor, were enough sermons in manuscript form for two, if not three, more volumes. These were written out longhand on the reverse side of discarded manuscripts (from books, articles, etc.) and halved so as to take into the pulpit as inconspicuous copy. Owing to the fact that Farrer seldom, if ever, preached except from a full manuscript, we have yet further examples of his rare literary and homiletical skills. I think the reader will agree that this collection forms a suitable complement to its predecessors.

I should like to thank: the Publisher and editors of SPCK and the Trustees of the Farrer estate for making this publication possible; the Reverend Leslie Houlden for his advice in connection with the manuscript; Miss E. Gill for reading the proofs; Dr A. L. Rowse for permission to reproduce his poem on Epstein's Lazarus; The Southern Fellowships Fund for their generous grant. Most of all, my indebtedness belongs to Katherine Farrer for letting me root about under the rafters.

Mansfield College
Oxford   CHARLES C. CONTI

INTRODUCTION

It is by now generally acknowledged that Austin Farrer was one of the great preachers of his generation—indeed, some of us would say, of any generation. In an age when rhetoric is mistrusted, he developed a new kind. He did not, like most public speakers, have lazy recourse to a flaccid colloquialism, or rattle off pages of that buff-coloured bureaucratese so much affected by those in all walks of life, clergy included, who hope to be thought sensible, practical men. His style was concrete, articulate, often beautiful, but above all acceptable, because it was suffused at its best with a delicacy that could be sensitive or light-hearted as the time required. It was a quiet, sometimes self-mocking rhetoric; but a rhetoric none the less. The style was so much the man; but it was a conscious style. He aimed to move his hearers, to play upon them, not for any false effects, but so that they might see and perceive, hear and understand, and turn again and be healed.

Published sermons present a special problem. They invite a literary judgement which may be thought irrelevant to the proper criterion for a sermon as such: namely, does it help its hearers to know God, Father, Son, and Holy Spirit, more clearly, love him more dearly, and follow him more nearly? Sermons no one would think of printing have saved souls; sermons much admired by posterity may have achieved nothing. But these very facts suggest that, once a sermon is printed, it ought to be approached, inevitably will be approached, with expectations different from those which we bring to the spoken word. In one sense there is no such thing as a printed 'sermon', *tout simple*. What we have is a rather subtle art-form in which the tightness of argument, precision and beauty of expression, and organization of structure which we look for in a literary piece are to be combined with the dramatic impression of the spoken word. This was an art much practised in antiquity: Pericles addressing the men of Athens, Peter's sermon to the Jews on the Day of Pentecost, are obvious and celebrated examples. What is rare indeed is that the text of a genuine sermon as actually delivered should satisfy the criteria of the literary form as well. To the tiny company of such preachers of genius Austin Farrer belongs.

We both may and should, therefore, approach these sermons as weighed and precise statements of theology and spirituality. They exemplify strikingly the way in which, in his later years, Austin Farrer was striving for new depths of simplicity and insight, for the words which would help us to see all God's dealings as of a piece—in short, to understand not merely God's activity as we experience it but God's nature, translucent, unified, and perfect. And the purpose of such understanding is worship. These sermons commonly turn at their close to some eucharistic theme; but whether the point is made explicit or not, they are all integrated into the liturgy, and are themselves acts of praise and adoration. The trinitarian ascription with which almost every sermon concludes is here no ecclesiastical convention. For Austin Farrer, it was the essential reason why he was in the pulpit at all.

This struggle for a unified simplicity of truth at its deepest level means inevitably that the attempt does not always come off. But even when it does not (as, I think, in 'Holy Feasts'), we are valuably stirred; and when it does——! What question could be tougher to handle honestly and profoundly within the confines of a sermon than that of our freedom and God's will? Certainly Austin Farrer was as highly qualified to handle it as any living man, as his Gifford Lectures bear witness. Yet many of the greatest lecturers would be baffled to find a way of conveying in fifteen minutes to a nonspecialist audience something of the insight which they would happily expound to adepts in fifteen hours. But we read 'The Privilege of Challenge'—and lo! the thing has been done. Or again, we turn to 'Fences and Friends', and the whole irritating puzzle of that 'justification' stuff is not only illumined but made fruitful for our good.

Throughout these sermons the reader will note certain recurring words and ideas which preoccupied the preacher's love and thought during these years: 'glory', 'light', 'man in the image of God', 'we have the mind of Christ'. Significantly, we are often brought back to the Prologue of St John's Gospel; and we notice too, more frequent and intense elements of poetry and mysticism.

But these features are balanced by a stinging concreteness and practicality in his pastoral teaching. His was a tough, old-fashioned morality—as shown, for example, in 'Money', or in 'Radical Piety'. Without any trace of vindictiveness or of holierthan-thou he does, in the old phrase, 'convict of sin', because he talks straight and hard to his congregation about their particular failures. Not for him the easy prophetism which whips up purely emotional horror at tyranny or poverty safe thousands of miles away. He tells his undergraduate congregations that if they are on bad terms with their parents, then it is their Christian duty to put that right as soon as they possibly can; that the heart of their life at University is their work, and that all the other splendid things must be fitted in round that. He pricks them about getting up in the morning, running into debt, writing home. It is plain that 'human respect', as Faber so searchingly analysed it, never got his tongue. He did not let the reflection, 'They will think I am a silly old schoolmaster, treating them like kids', unnerve him. But Austin Farrer's glory as a pastoral preacher was that he could make such rebukes acceptable, and therefore productive, not just by 'touching it light' but because he set the particular fault or virtue in such a wide and wonderful context. The listener was helped to see that at this small point nothing less than the cosmic and re-deeming love of God could find expression. And that is why all readers, even though their sins may have changed since they were eighteen or twenty, can benefit. We are helped to think and feel about all sin and goodness in the right way by these needle-sharp examples.

One sermon in this book shows the preacher's down-to-earth honesty in an unexpected light. This is the one entitled 'On Being an Anglican'. Austin Farrer is so much in the classic tradition of Christendom that one thinks of him as not of a church but for all the Body of Christ. And this is true. But he was what he was in a characteristically Anglican way; and he believed passionately in the rightness of belonging to the Church of England. This belief he expresses here in language which today comes as something of a shock to us who are enjoying the chumminess of a still rather new ecumenical courtesy. But the shock is salutary. We shall have to get back to the question of truth one day.

Two final observations. First, the sermons are again marked with those characteristic Austinian strokes of genius that so delighted us in earlier collections: the way Bethlehem is brought in in 'Caprice'; the imperceptible move from a student's choice of subject to God's choice of Incarnation ('Consecrated Bread').

There are also the amusing but fundamentally serious observations of life, as in his remarks on faces in 'Physical Faith'. But above all the preacher succeeds by turning things completely round, by saying to us: 'You are getting all bothered about this because you are looking at it from the wrong end.' A classic example comes in 'Rewards and Punishments'. And of course the joy is that once we grasp the principle, we can with growing effectiveness use it to open our own lives to the transforming grace of God.

Secondly, it is plain that for Austin Farrer, venerate as he did Paul or John or any great Christian, the fountainhead of life and truth is Christ. He was as acquainted as any man with the 'problem of the historical Jesus'; but he was absolutely clear that this did not cut us off from knowing Jesus, the 'dear man', as in essentials he was and as in substance he taught. Today there are powerful voices which seem bent on making Jesus a nominal figurehead. We need Austin Farrer's clear judgement, strong common sense, and inspired love for his Lord, as our ally in what may well be this generation's decisive battle for the soul of Christianity and the hope of the world.

Corpus Christi College, Oxford   JOHN AUSTIN BAKER

The End of Man

PREACHED IN PUSEY HOUSE OXFORD 1966

What happens if you put a pair of rabbits on a desert island? Supposing, that is, the island is really desert, quite empty of animal life: no foxes, for instance, no buzzards. Well, the rabbits multiply and they eat the grass. You might think that when the grass won't support any more rabbits, the colony stops increasing merrily and the population stabilizes. Not a bit of it. They all begin to starve on the same day, they all get deficiency diseases, and all but a handful of them die. Indeed they may all die: then there's an end of rabbits.

The globe is our rabbit-island. There are no buzzards or foxes to keep the human rabbits down. It has taken us all these millennia to reach global capacity; we're nearly there. When there is nothing more to eat, we are not so likely all to die of deficiency diseases; we are more likely all to blow one another to bits. And so there'll be an end of man. The writers of science fiction do not find the possibility amusing—for annihilation is annihilation, and about nothing there is nothing to be said. So they save a handful of their human rabbits, to be the Noah's Ark of a universe and start a new round of history. But suppose there is no Noah's Ark: suppose the destruction is complete—how much does it matter, if there's an end of man?

But before we consider that portentous question, let's give the science fiction writers their heads. We will agree then that the handful of humans survive, but in what form? Their genetic character is greatly affected by nuclear fall-out. Never mind, nature copes somehow, and, with a violent mutation, settles into a new biological balance. The human race survives, but the human creature is unrecognizable for what it was; suppose anything you like—we walk on our hands, we see with our ears, we hear with our noses. Our passions and feelings become quite differently balanced; we see the world upside down and ourselves inside out. Meanwhile we excavate the ruins of the Oxford science area, recover the brilliant discoveries of the twentieth century, and go forward so to elaborate our material civilization that life becomes a completely different affair from what it was. We look back on the records of previous centuries and find the activities of former men no nearer to us than those of bees and ants. What has happened? Men have admittedly had descendants: but are these creatures men? Could we come to the end of man, and go on into something else?

So there are two possibilities: we blow one another up without remainder, and there's an end of man. Or we go on to the end of man, and after; for if we become another animal altogether, then there's an end of man; just as there's an end of an under-graduate, when he takes his degree; though not in the same sense as there's an end of one if, failing to take his degree, he takes his life.

Either way, there could be an end of man. But then on either supposition, what about THE END OF MAN: the end, that is, for which he was created? For the end of man is not just that he should come to an end; any more than it is the end for which a violin is made, to be jumped upon by a hooligan: but that it should play sweet music. On either of our sensational alternatives, when man ends, will the end of man have been achieved; will the human music have been played?

It is fortunate that philosophy lecturers do not attend Pusey House sermons, for were such a man here, he would be boiling in his seat. 'Do we not tell our pupils,' he mutters, 'ten times a year that comparisons between artefacts and living creatures are utterly fallacious?' An instrument is made to do a job. Very well then: that's its end. Living creatures have no end prescribed to them except that they should live. They themselves create ends by adopting pursuits. There is no such thing as the end of man: the ends of men are what they make them.

Very well; nothing has an end, unless it has a maker: and if we were atheists perhaps there'd be no more we could say; for then we should not think we had a maker. All the same we have. Certainly he does not make us as a man makes a machine; and so our relation to our end will not be like that of a machine. A machine is limited to a fixed end. But in fact we took the example of a violin, of which the ends are not fixed, but in a manner open and infinite. True, a violin will only play violin-music; but cannot we vary and enrich the music for ever? There is no end of the music, no end to the fiddler's art, the violin has an end which is endless.

So with the end of man. To speak of 'the end of man', as a Christian speaks of it, is not to speak of fulfilling that biological existence which we share with slugs and snails, or even with plants and trees. The nerves, the fingers and the throats of men form a complex instrument on which the discourse of reason can be played; action can be thought, and thought can be enacted; and thought is more truly endless even than music, for it has more dimensions. Why, musical composition is itself one of the forms of thought: and how many more there are!

So then, either our supposed new race can think, or it cannot. If it cannot, then it will not be able to pursue THE END OF MAN. But if it can, then whatever happens to its physical constitution, or to its cultural pattern, it can continue to pursue that glorious end.

Thought is unlimited in its nature, though the bodily fiddle on which we play that music is so limited. Thought can go anywhere, and so can the passion and the desire which accompany it. So the end of man is not fixed by the instrument with which he thinks, nor by the heart with which he loves. The universe is ours in which to expatiate, to spread ourselves. Our end is fixed not by our faculties, but by what there is most worthy to be loved and known; and that is God, God in himself, God in all his infinite works and ways. For all knowing is a knowledge of God, and all loving is a loving of him, where there is purity of heart.

So then, if they have hearts to love what is lovely in itself, and minds to contemplate without coveting, our imaginary grand-children will have undergone no change which frustrates THE END OF MAN, whatever happens to the shape of their bodies or the pattern of their lives.

Ah, but suppose the fiction of our novelists to be false; suppose no human handful survives the global war; suppose the race perishes without remainder: then surely the end of man has been snapped off short and never once attained: God's providence must acknowledge defeat. Yes, if God's heart is set upon a never-ending progeny of human souls. But why should we suppose so? Perhaps he will have had enough. After all, it does not take a nuclear war to make death universal. Death is universal; and none of us attains THE END OF MAN before he dies. Let the race perish from the earth: all those who have been saved in Christ are made alive with him, and proceed to the possession of that infinite good which here they blindly sought. God is the end of man, and God is not seen in this life, but at the best believed, even by the pure in heart.

The most insidious error of our severe philosophical theologians is to set aside the life to come as a thing indifferent, a matter of no concern, which Christians may or may not believe. What? Do we see God in this life? Is it a matter of no concern, a thing indifferent, whether we are ever to attain our only end? If it is indifferent to our earth-bound thoughts, is it indifferent to the heart of God? They think too meanly of his love to us who call this hope in question. Belief in this infinite and invaluable gift, this partaking of God's eternity, is the acid test of genuine faith. Leave this out of account, and you can equivocate for ever on God's very existence: your talk about God can always be talk about the backside of nature, dressed in emotional rhetoric. But a God who reverses nature, a God who undoes death, that those in whom the likeness of his glory has faintly and fitfully shone may be drawn everlastingly into the heart of light, and know him as he is: this is a God indeed, a God Almighty, a God to be trusted, loved, adored.

The end of man is endless Godhead endlessly possessed, but that end flows back in glory on our mortal days, and gives a hope and meaning to whatever Christians do for love of God or love of one another. For we are all heirs of everlastingness, and whatever we do or are furnishes material to the hands which out of perishing stuff create eternal joy.

We cannot, in this life, wholly possess the end we pursue; for man cannot reach his end, until there is an end of man—until we cease from self, and turn outwards on God and on the children of God. And such self-forgetfulness is not attained in a mortal body. Flesh and blood, says Christ's apostle, cannot attain the kingdom of God. See, I show you a mystery—all need not sleep the sleep of death, but all must undergo this change, though it be in the twinkling of an eye, at the last trump. For the trumpet shall sound, and the dead shall be raised incorruptible, and we shall be changed. For this corruptible being must put on incorruption, and this mortal put on immortality. And Christ himself more simply said, 'He that would gain his life must lose it.' So there must be an end of man, that man may possess his everlasting end and, emptied of himself, be filled with God. All must be caught up and transformed in that death and resurrection which Christ fulfilled for us, and to which he unites us through this sacrament, the medicine and the pledge of immortality.

Preached during Hilary Term 1966, as part of a course on the theme: 'Christian Faith and Practice'.

The Death of Death

PREACHED IN KEBLE COLLEGE CHAPEL OXFORD 1968

We are all mortal; and so it is no use a clergyman's treating it as a matter of surprise, that occasions for him to read the burial service are not infrequent. If a man had a parish of 24,000, he might expect to bury one a day. I do not want you to work out the arithmetical basis of that calculation, for if you are so occupied you will not be listening to what I want to tell you. If the priest works the sum, his arithmetic can remove from his mind any surprise he might feel at the frequency of such ceremonies; but nothing (it may be) will cure him of the surprise with which he finds himself, time after time, assuring the mourners on the authority of St Paul that we shall not all sleep the sleep of death, but we shall all be transformed, in a moment, in the twinkling of an eye, at the last trump: so that we, who have hitherto led a flesh-and-blood existence, will be changed into the substance of glory.

I do not know how useful it is to relay St Paul's speculation to the Christian mourners of today, but I do think it is worthwhile our reflecting on it, just because it involves us—creatures of flesh and blood—in a head-on collision with Omnipotence. No doubt we think, or half think, we have to undergo such a collision in a disembodied state, when there will be no more evasion, and we meet Truth himself face to face.

But when we think of this, our imaginations are not moved: for we have a hazy feeling that anything might happen to a disembodied spirit: we know not what we shall be and for all we know meeting with deity may be all in the day's work then. But the mental shock is real, if we conceive of ourselves such as we now are undergoing that divine encounter. What would happen? St Paul says, we should be changed: and we do not need to go outside those few words, to touch the height of amazement. We should be changed: changed—and how? St Paul speaks of the seed corn changed into the plant of wheat, and others, more appropriately perhaps, have talked of the chrysalis becoming a moth or the larva a dragonfly. I once lay in a punt on the Cherwell, spellbound for an hour, watching the dragonfly miracle; and indeed it was amazing enough. Yet it certainly did not happen in the twinkle of an eye, but through an agony of birth: slow, yes, agonizingly slow. Nor was it a miracle, after all, for it was all in the way of nature: the expansion of what had been folded, the liberation of what had been compressed. For in the works of nature God works naturally; that there should be dragonflies at all, not to mention men, is a breath-taking wonder, if we think of those mere rudiments of being from which such creatures are evolved—not surely without a power divine. Yet the Creator's will has waited ages for such things to work themselves out by the action of inborn energies, under the infinitely subtle and unforced persuasion of invisible providence.

But *then*, says St Paul, in the twinkling of an eye, we shall be changed: God will no longer wait for the ripening of nature nor restrict his action within nature's bounds: for this is where nature ends. We shall be changed, in the twinkling of an eye, for all this bodily being of ours will utterly melt at the touch of our maker and offer not a moment's resistance to his purest thought, his most absolute will; suddenly our being will become the simple print of his intention for us.

You and I may pray, as our Saviour taught us, *Thy will be done*, and wish we may be wax in the hands of Almighty Love; and Mercy will accept our true desire, while knowing how slow is the ripening of our virtue and how many obstacles the coarseness of our flesh and blood opposes to our maker's purpose. But it will be otherwise when we are changed, in the twinkling of an eye; then God will have his way with us, and to experience this will be to know God indeed. For the invisible Creator is known to his creatures in his creating of them: and when he freely and without obstacle fashions us, he will be perfectly known, felt as it were in the pressure of his fingers and read in the expression of his creative thoughts. Shall not we be ourselves the embodied thoughts of God, when we are changed?

But what are we doing? We've let St Paul's speculation run away with us. Is nature to melt in the rays of insupportable light that God may be all in all? Not, perhaps, without first passing through a natural death: perhaps in spite of St Paul, we all shall sleep, before we are any of us changed. Certainly, whatever St Paul may have thought, he slept the sleep of death, he and all the

generation he addressed; they did not hear in this world the blast
of the archangel, the trump of God.

Still, we needn't be too hard on the Apostle. How was he to
know the very form and timing of events yet to come? He was
bound to think that some day, and in some way, the whole being
of the saints must become glass to God's thoughts and wax to his
will. So much for looking forward—and then, as for looking backward, he had seen it happen. Had he not seen the Lord, the risen
Lord? At one point nature and history had melted in the immediate ray of power. A body was laid in the tomb, a living, speaking
glory issued from it.

To think with meaning of Christ's resurrection we must look
behind the world; for from within the world such an event is
supremely unnatural. We must dare to look into God, and see how
no created thing is at all, but by his will. And *then* what may seem
unnatural is the way in which God gives created nature rights
against himself and shapes his will on her slow, groping motives.
How natural, that Almighty Purpose should simply prevail; how
natural that nature's rights should be withdrawn: how natural,
how inevitable, that God at length should gather the harvest of
his patience, and that, in the ray of immortal light, we should be
changed: that something created should be as he would have it.

But when? Looking forward, St Paul hoped to know but did not
know. Looking backward, he knew. Once there had been nothing
God should wait for; when a life was lived, and a death died, in
simple self-offering to God, that God's love for all the world might
be achieved. When we shall melt in the will of God to be re-
fashioned, it will be the pain of fire, says St Paul, so attached are we
to the darling self we love, so fearful of the God who kills to make
alive. Not so the resurrection of Christ. The killing had all been
done already: there was nothing he had not offered up, nothing
that had not been dissolved in his natural being, when his conscious mind was reduced to a snatch of verse just floating over the
rising oblivion, *Eli, Eli, lama sabachthani*. The killing had all
been done; how then should the making alive be withheld?
Would not the Son's perfect sacrifice have forced the Father's
hand, if that had needed any forcing. Ah, no; what can be more
covetous of opportunity than God's immortal love, his life-giving
grace? He flows in like the tide to fill every cranny that opens: re-

pent, and in a moment he has filled your heart. Christ's sacrifice was completed in his burial, and in a twinkling of an eye he was changed.

And now, do you see, I have scarcely overtaken what was supposed to be my starting-point: what has Christ done for us by his resurrection? What for us? But nothing one can say on this subject is much better than silence: what shall we say? He has given us the substance of glory. Being changed in God, he is the heart of heaven and he draws us into association with himself: the action of the man-in-God, the God-in-man, is an action he shares with us and entrusts to us. We have yet to be changed, to melt in the will of God—and even so, we already possess by association, and by attachment to Christ, that victorious and transfigured life after which we aspire. Our end is unchangeably far—our fusion in God, our new-creation. And yet in Christ it is near, it is possessed: if any man be in Christ, he is—not shall be, but is—a new creation.

Ah—but like ignorant children, making toys of their mother's jewels, or like postal sorters passing packets and not thinking what they contain, we handle our only treasure, the pearl of great price, and scarcely regard it. But that is not the matter of any single sermon, that is every sermon. Think what you have—be what you are—take your paradise.

The Christ of resurrection did inspire and may inspire terror, for he is what we shall be on the other side of the fire, and we fear the fire. Yet we read that the fear of the disciples turned to familiarity and kindness, for whatever the risen Christ be in himself he came to meet them and returned into the place and into the forms of flesh and blood; he talked, he listened, he gave himself to be touched, he shared their food. For the man-in-God, the man utterly molten and fashioned in God's will, is not separated, not fenced off from us. How would that serve the loving will of which he is made the sensitive instrument? We fear the fire—yet all the fire will do will be to make us happy in living out the love of God; and Jesus, who needed no fire beyond the suffering of his passion, was moved by love to return among his disciples as the dear man they had known; and our painter, whatever you may think of his art, was no fool in the thoughts he conceived, when he showed our Saviour on his rounds in human guise, patiently knocking at the doors of our hearts.*

* A reference to 'The Light of the World', by Holman Hunt, in the Lady Chapel of Keble.

The Brink of Mystery

Perhaps in these humanist days it will be proper to begin with a text from Voltaire:

> Why did Jeremiah's tears
> Overflow his earthly years?
> Did his prophet-heart advise him
> How our panel would revise him?

It would, indeed, be intriguing to have back the dead, and hear what they have to say about our transformations of their works, or their ideas, or their customs. What would the fathers of the American Republic have to say about the modern form of presidential election? What would Dante say of Miss Sayers's translations from his *Commedia*? And what would a primitive Christian say about our keeping of Holy Week? There are (St Paul admits) those who esteem one day as more important than another; but these are weak consciences, who have never quite managed to get the Jewish ecclesiastical calendar out of their systems. A Christian will keep Sunday, no doubt, as the day on which our Sun of Righteousness rose upon us from the tomb, with healing in his wings. And Easter Day? Yes, if you like; what's the odds? Easter is just the typical Sunday, and Sunday means exactly what Easter means. Friday? No, name it not: Friday was the seeming triumph of Antichrist. Certainly our God turned that triumph into a defeat; but this is exactly what we celebrate on Sunday: the cross and God's transformation of the cross. When, then, will you read the story of the Passion? Oh, we will begin our Sunday on the eve, and read it then. Well, we reply to our apostolic Christian, do you see any fatal objections to our lengthening the Eve of Easter backwards into a vigil covering Holy Week? Glory be to God, he replies, I venerate your austerity. You will surely grow hungry by the seventh day. No, no, we say; we eat hot cross buns, and other things. We fast in a much more spiritual manner: we fill our minds with the sorrow of the Passion. Oh, you do, do you? says he. And what is the good of that? The Syrian girls wail for Thammuz, and

the unbelieving Jews manage to tremble and quake ten days from
New Year to Atonement. I thought that the Sun of Joy had risen
upon us, and himself commanded us, when we fast, to keep a cheerful countenance. He died for us, indeed; but is he sorry to have
done it? No. There is nothing he is happier to have done, than
this. Did not he, in the generosity of his love, give himself away
to us with his own hands, in bread to be eaten, and wine to be
drunk?

It's all very well for you to talk, we may still protest, but you
haven't tried living in modern New York, or London, or Rio.
Nothing happens in these places that can't be listed under one of
three heads—the lust of the eyes, the lust of the flesh, and the
boast of life. We must get away at set seasons (or we never shall)
and live ourselves back into the mystery of our redemption.
Very well, our ancient replies, but into the *whole* of the mystery,
please. If the aim is to keep the vigil of the Feast, and prepare
yourselves for Easter, think about Easter. You won't do much
thinking *after* Easter, I guess. So if you think about nothing but
the Passion in Holy Week, you will never get round to contem-
plating the divine victory at all.

When we have reached this point in the conversation, or shall I
say, the séance, I look past the nameless shade who has been
answering me, and see a man with a lion's head embroidered on
his tunic, and a book in his hand. I peer at the book he carries,
half expecting to see it torn, or damaged at the last page. What?
I say to the venerable Evangelist, so your gospel is complete,
after all? Yes, says St Mark: I wrote no more. The women ran
from the tomb, and held their tongues: it was not their report
which set the glorious gospel in motion. There was no need for
me to tell the Church that Jesus, risen as he had promised, sent
his apostles forth into all the world.

Well, if you take that line, I reply, there was no need for you to
tell the Church anything: the Church knows. We thought you had
written your book to help the Church know what she knows,
placarding Christ before her very eyes, and pouring the word of
life into her ears. Where is your gospel of the resurrection?

How shall I make you see the resurrection? he replied. I show
you, in all my book, the kingship of God present in the action of a
man. To die is human; to rise again is divine. I can make you feel

the nerve of heroic death; it is a human possibility, you can see yourself called upon to face martyrdom too—in my day we had all to face it. And though you would not hope to conquer without divine grace, you know what it is to live in grace; and what it would be to call on grace, as you wait to die. But to rise again from death—it does not lie with any man to do that, however assisted by heaven. It is not a human action: it is nothing but a touch of the finger of God.

What is it, then? St Mark continues: I can show you—I *have* shown you—God in man defeating death, by dying. It is a story as much human as it is divine. The rest is not a story, and I cannot tell it—not, that is, the story of Jesus, and what it was for him to rise from the dead. Of course, I can tell—others will doubtless tell—the story of his disciples, and what it was for them to be shone upon by the new light of Christ's resurrection; for in that story we all of us still live, if we are Christians indeed. Not that we have all seen the Lord, as Peter saw him, or as Paul—these were apostles. I was only an under-worker with the gospel. I followed, alas, with hesitant steps; but I wrote what I heard.

So, then, if we are to believe St Mark's shade—or, for that matter, if we are to believe St Mark's writing as we have it—there is some reason for the concentration of our worship on the groaning cross, rather than on the bursting tomb. It is not that the penal atonement is more central to our faith than the victorious life; or that we should dwell on a death to sin, and merely hope for a resurrection to righteousness. No, our religion is the victorious life, but that victory is seen more in the humanity of the passion than in the divinity of the resurrection. Truly, Christ risen is human, still; but our clue to that humanity is the life he suffered in our flesh and blood, not the felicity he enjoys in the substance of his glory.

There is a traditional and quite simple form of prayer, or shall we say of private worship, which consists of taking gospel scenes, and living oneself into them. There is even a traditional and quite limited set of scenes: the joys of Christmas, the sorrows of Holy Week, the glories from Easter into heaven itself. Now to take the first group. We cannot enter into the joys of Christ's birth, except through the eyes of a witness. We cannot be Jesus in his annunciation and nativity, we can only be Mary. And the same is true of Christ's resurrection, and ascension, and his sending of the Spirit. We cannot, even in devout imagination, be Christ doing these things; we can only be Mary, or one of the disciples, witnessing them. But in the mysteries of the Passion we might go further. We might dare, in contemplation, to see and feel the event not as Mary or John, but as Jesus feels and sees it; to speak, with his lips, to his Father; to care, with his heart, for his friends; to join him in forgiving his enemies; in his tortured limbs, if we dare, to encounter his death. We can follow him to the brink of mystery, we can touch the gates of victory with his dying hands. We cannot open them; he could not. It is as far as man can go. The rest is God.

It cannot be wrong, whatever our apostolic ghost may have said —it cannot be wrong for a Christian to identify himself with the heart of Christ, and specially in his passion. We make the identification—or we ask him to take us into it. We do not set out to be sorry, or to turn on any tap of feeling rather than any other— how could we be so profane? We go with the action of Christ, content to feel or to feel nothing, to sorrow or to rejoice, as may befall. There is only one movement of the heart that is vital— that we should love; and this will be be given, not self-induced. There is no recipe for love, but looking at the force in the heart which moves it.

If anyone wishes to go into the heart of Christ, he has an easy door. There will be no difficulty about seeing God in heaven, we shall look into thoughts as clear as crystal; and yet never see to the bottom of the well. And though we shall never see to the bottom of Christ's heart, we can always see into it as far as our penetration reaches. For Jesus is the most candid, the most single and entire of men who ever lived. Whatever he says, he exactly means: whatever he does has *all* his heart in it. He does not forgive his torturers because he thinks it fit; he forgives them. His intention is an absolute simplicity—it is the intention to forgive. The difficulty we have of representing it to ourselves is like the difficulty of calling up before our memory the scent of a flower, the tone of a bell, or a colour in the rainbow. Each is clear and translucent: there is nothing shaded or subtle in any of them; it is just that imagination has not the colours in her box to do them justice, or to give them force. When Christ forgives, he forgives—it is our forgiveness, not his, that is full of subtleties and shades of meaning. His is entire. We cannot reach the candour of it.

What was I saying? The heart of Christ is wide open, it sounds in his words and shines in his acts: we can look straight in, though we cannot reach the depth of it. There is plenty there for our meditation, and especially in the history of his passion; where love is shown stronger than death, and many waters cannot quench the fire.

If we meditate the passion through the heart of Jesus, we may, perhaps, achieve the main purpose of our exercise—that of getting on the right side of the battle. It is better, as even Gamaliel saw, to fight on God's side, than to fight against him. The great sin or error of Caiaphas and Pilate and Judas Iscariot is that they were opposing the purpose of almighty love: and it will be small consolation to them on the day of Judgement to claim that their action was justifiable by political, moral or religious rules. It was—but they fought against God; and we do not want to spend our lives doing this. So, by finding out where Jesus was, we will hope to find out where he is, and to adhere to him, and stick by him, rather than, while we frustrate his purpose, to be justified at the bar of any legal judgement. At the great Assize of God, Pilate and Caiaphas will find small comfort in the extenuations that can fairly be offered for their all too natural actions. What will console them will be the discovery, that though they fought against God, they did not prevail; and when they seemed to have crushed his kingdom, they were putting victory into his hands. But more than this it will console them, that, if they can be reconciled, they are forgiven.

Physical Faith

Thomas said to his fellow disciples:

Except I shall see in his hands
the prints of the nails and
put my finger into the print of the nails,
and thrust my hand into his side,
I will not believe. JOHN 20.25

This is the Easter Faith: God is the conqueror. Outside and beyond the bounds of this life, in a way we cannot pretend to conceive, his creative power conquers our decay. What sin has rotted and age has atrophied, he will make again a new man: new, and yet the same. He will bestow on this new man the fellowship of all the saints and the vision of his own face. And our faith in this miracle is to overcome the evidence of our senses—we are to look on the utter destruction, the blank non-entity of death, and see through to the miracle of resurrection on the other side, on a shore we have never observed nor can even point to, for it is neither up nor down nor before nor behind. And to this miracle we must look, not merely as our comfort in the face of death, but as the mark by which we are to strive all our life long and towards which we are to strain our whole aspiration. And of the truth of this, God has given us our only sufficient pledge: what he will do for all in the end and out of this world, he did for Jesus in this world and as it were by anticipation.

Why all this rhetoric? I was looking the other day at a friend of mine, dying slowly and painfully and not at all old. As Hamlet's uncle remarked, the experience is common: we deceive ourselves if we suppose our friends are physically immortal.

This is the Christian faith—and what other faith is even a faith at all? How can you believe in a God who does not make his saving will finally effective, and how can he unless he raises the dead? If death is left the master of the field, what spoils can saving love retain? Death is a clean sweep.

So to believe less than this is to believe nothing; our faith, says

St Paul, is vain if Christ did not rise. But to believe this—Do I believe? Ought I to be terribly candid, and to say I don't believe? But should I be candid to say so? Anyhow, let me be candid—as candid as St Thomas. 'St Thomas the doubter' we say; but to make St Thomas a typical doubter is to miss the point of his character: there is no agnosticism about him, no hesitancy, no balancing of pros and cons, no sitting on the fence. He speaks right out. When Jesus had proposed to go back into Judea, in spite of the Jewish threat to his life, it was St Thomas who had blurted out, 'Let us go too, and die with him.' You see how he stripped the last wrapping from the menacing facts, how he drew the hard, practical consequence for his fellow-disciples and himself: 'Let us go too, then, and die with him.' He showed the same directness and simplicity at the Last Supper, when the discourse of Jesus outran his disciples' comprehension. Jesus had said, 'You know the road where I am going.' 'No we don't,' said Thomas. 'We don't know where you are going, to start with; so how can we know which road to take?' If only all we who try to teach had such downright pupils as St Thomas, ready to own up as soon as they lose the thread of the lesson! But we have made our pupils too timid, or too polite: they let us go on pouring our words into the empty air.

St Thomas was just as open, just as downright when it came to believing or disbelieving Christ's resurrection. He had been absent when Christ first appeared in the upper room: the twelve gave him the news. 'It is no good,' said he, 'I shan't believe unless I put my finger into the print of the nails.' Here was a man who knew his own mind. There is no reason to suppose that he is being wilful or perverse. He is not saying, 'Unless I see and touch, I *refuse* to believe,' as though he could believe perfectly well if he liked. He is saying, 'There's no hope of my believing a thing like that, unless my eyes and hands convince me. I'm sorry, but that's the way I am. How am I to know you weren't just seeing visions?'

That was the sort of man St Thomas was about believing and disbelieving. They are more blessed, said Christ, who do not need such brutal evidence as the exploring of wounds with a finger; blessed are they who have not seen, and yet have believed. Nevertheless, Christ had mercy on St Thomas, he acknowledged the honesty of his disbelief, and took extreme measures to meet and overcome it: 'Reach hither thy finger, and observe my hand; reach hither thy hand, and put it in my side, and be not faithless, but believing.' But Thomas had had enough. 'My Lord and my God,' he said.

What Christ did and said on that occasion shows his mercy to us all. He has salvation for believers and disbelievers both: take whichever part applies to you. Have you the happy faith of St Peter and St John, who rose and ran to the sepulchre at St Mary Magdalen's word, who saw no angels, only the empty grave-clothes, and yet believed? If you have such a faith, then to you belongs the blessing: 'Happy are they who believe not having seen.' But if you are a disbeliever like St Thomas, than this is for you, this is Christ's mercy to you: 'Reach hither your finger and observe my hand, thrust your hand into my side, and be not faithless, but believing.'

St Thomas is not praised for disbelieving: if he had been more open-eyed to all Christ's wondrous works, more attentive to his life-giving words throughout his ministry, perhaps he need not have disbelieved at the last. He is not praised for disbelieving, but still less would he have been praised if he had pretended to believe, if he had tried to fool his fellow-disciples; still worse, if he had tried to fool his own mind. He confessed his disbelief with all possible candour, and so Christ came to his relief, as previously he had come to the relief of that other who cried: 'Lord, I believe; help thou mine unbelief.'

We may take St Thomas as our patron while candour is what we require. One thing at a time: some day perhaps you will follow St John into the blessedness of a perfect belief, but today you may join St Thomas and know what you believe and what you do not; that is the first step. Our Christendom is rotted away with pretended belief, insincere belief, until we do not know what we believe; until, indeed, we lose the very sense of what believing is, or of what the difference is between belief and disbelief.

Candour is a rare virtue. If you want to know men's characters, do not listen to their words, nor pay too much attention to their faces while they are speaking to you. Look at their faces in repose, when they are unaware of being observed: then you can often see them exactly as they are. Do not hesitate to draw the consequences of what you see: that self-conceit, that discontent, that greediness, that ill-will is the prevailing attitude of the man; or again, that sweetness, that resignation, that mysterious radiance which the love of God pours upon the face of the saints. But—and here I am not speaking of the saints, but of the others—do not suppose that when the man comes alive and begins to display towards you a conventional amiability, he is consciously deceiving you. He is deceiving himself. He does not accept the evidence of that unpleasant mask which catches him sometimes in the looking-glass before he has had time to grin. He thinks he really holds all the conventionally amiable principles and attitudes which are displayed in his polite conversation. He thinks he is what he says. He does not know those deep grounds of belief or disbelief which inspire all his important actions and square with all his prevalent desires. You may know them better than he does, just by watching his face in his unguarded moments. I do not see myself, my neighbour sees my face, and God—God sees my heart. What does my neighbour see on my reposing face? What is written there? Misplaced confidence in my own cleverness, or humble trust in God? A closed concentration on my own pursuits, or an open affection towards men? Moses wore a mask to hide the glory of God shining on his face; the mask I wear hides very different things. Yet wear it as I may, it steps sideways and betrays me even to mankind, while the eyes of God look straight through it into my heart. But I cannot deceive even my neighbour. The person whom I can really deceive is myself, for it is I alone who long to be deceived. My neighbour does not want to be deceived, he wants to know me as I am. But I do not want to know myself as I am.

There's no question about it, we ought not to lie so much as we do. That sounds a childish thing to say. But we have a doctrine about white lies, about tactful, charitable lies, about amusing lies, which we have stretched so far, that we have corrupted the integrity of our minds; so that we talk no longer for the purpose of revealing either the truth of fact or the truth of feeling: we talk to amuse, to flatter, to impress, to mislead. If people take us seriously, the more fools they. Our policy recoils upon us: we no longer know what we think, believe or feel. In a Christian discussion-meeting, we express pious and orthodox sentiments; in the street, cynical and worldly sentiments. Now what *are* our sentiments? The pious sentiments are what we think we *ought* to believe; the cynical sentiments are what it would be *amusing* to believe: but neither is what we *do* believe.

Never mind, we shall soon find out, for here we are going to pray. Now we are going into the presence of him before whom there are no disguises. Now we shall be sincere. No, nothing of the kind: even here we shall dissemble, for we have been taught that prayer is an exercise of faith. So what do we do? We get all the things that we think we ought to believe out of the cupboard, and pretend (with all our might) to believe them. What is the use of that? Is God pleased to hear us lying so hard, and are we edified by doing it?

Prayer is certainly an exercise of faith, but of the faith we have, not the faith we never had. Rather let me reveal before God all the nakedness of my spirit. O my God, I will say, I have scarcely believed. I have not lived out my beliefs, and so they are weak and vanishing. Of all the truth thou hast brought thy Church, how little means anything to me. And I have not deserved that it should be otherwise, for I have been unfaithful. Yet, O my God, thou hast not let me altogether disbelieve. If I said I disbelieved in thee, my God, I should be a liar and ungrateful, for thou hast given me belief. I believe that thou art in Jesus, in the church of Jesus, though I have not exercised myself to know how. Teach me in thy good time, O Lord, to enter more into the truth which thou hast revealed. But today the faith thou hast given me is enough. I throw myself upon thee, content to know that the faith thou hast given me is the presence and action of thy Holy Spirit. I leave everything to thee: thou wilt not let me fall.

If you deny your faith, you lie, and if you pretend that it is fuller than it is, you lie. A man's faith seems to a man himself to be the least possible link that could hold on to God, and yet it holds. Throw all your weight upon it, and it will grow strong in proportion to the strain.

St Thomas told no lies. He believed some things, but he did not, at that time, believe Christ's resurrection. Then Christ gave him his body to be the proof: and he gives us his body to be the proof. Christ's body is still in the world, his body is his faithful people. It was not every part of Christ's body that equally convinced St Thomas, it was the parts that carried the prints of the crucifixion. And it is not every part of Christ's body now that convinces us, it is the crucified parts: not every member of Christ, not every common Christian, but the saints who are marked with the signs of Christ's sacrifice. There are such men in the world, and we have known them: men whose words are like their faces and their faces like their hearts, and their hearts printed with the cross of Jesus. Jesus made them what they are, his death and resurrection is manifest in them. We have known them, let us not forget them: and may he who taught St Thomas take hold of our groping hands, and guide them to the prints of his saving wounds, where they can be seen and felt in the lives of Christ's true servants and saints; that in them we may acknowledge and glorify him who alone is worthy of all glory; to whom with the Father and the Holy Ghost be ascribed as is most justly due all might, dominion, majesty and power, henceforth and for ever.

First preached at St Thomas's, Regent Street, London, on that saint's day.

The Generous Eye

I suppose every thoughtful person has asked himself what there is so special about us human beings. You can say, of course, that we have immortal souls, and the animals have not. That's easy; in fact, it's a bit too easy. Gin and water is different from water, for you can taste the gin. Animal *plus* soul should be different from mere animal: you should be able to taste the soul. But can you? How does this extra thing, soul, display itself or make itself felt? Men are cleverer than animals, but animals can be quite clever too: it seems to be only a difference of degree. Getting cleverer and cleverer does not seem at all the same as graduating into immortality. Men, indeed, can love selflessly: but so can animals. I looked from my study window this morning, and there was a blackbird, pecking about among the garden-plants. Presently, with every symptom of delight, she fishes up a shining worm. Lucky blackbird! But no!—lucky fledgeling! For she flies straight under the syringa bush, where there is a great clumsy youngster fresh from the nest; into whose beak she delivers the spoil. Ah, you'll say, but men are capable of better things: aesthetic delight, artistic invention. Well, I do not say that thrush over there is a Bach or a Mozart, but how can I doubt that the song he sings is poured from the well of pure delight, or how can I deny the skill with which he turns and voices his phrase?

Certainly we shall not be better Christians for denying the excellence of any of God's creatures—they are all his handiwork. And yet God is specially to be praised in his most excellent works, and it is said of man alone, that God made him in his own image, after his very likeness. So what, after all, is that special likeness to God, which men have above the beasts? Is it not the power to get outside our skins, and see things impartially? God sees us all, just exactly as we are. God does not see things from a special God-point of view, as though he had a private interest or a personal prejudice. His vision is the truth. He sees what we are, and knows it; he sees what is sound in us and loves it; he sees what is good for us, and wills it. Animals are not like this. They see the world as it affects themselves: they love and hate their fellow-creatures only in so far as they touch them.

We men are also animals: every one of us inside his own skin, every one of us the centre of his own little world. And yet we also have a touch of the divine. When our selfish passions are cool, we have some power of getting outside ourselves, of standing in thought, on the very steps of God's throne, and looking down, as it were with God's impartial eyes, to see our own bodies crowding among the other bodies on the earth. We are able (to put it in more homely language) to recognize that each of us is only one pebble on the beach and that the claims of the other pebbles are equal to our own. In this way, we share in the *thought* of God. But to share in his *heart* comes harder: not only to acknowledge others' rights equally with our own, but to desire their good equally with our own. Divine sonship calls us out of ourselves; animal nature pulls us back into ourselves.

And so (as St Paul says) our sonship to God, our divine likeness, is something hidden, that has yet to be brought out and made plain. It is something bound down and enslaved, that struggles to be liberated. Like a mother agonizing to bring forth her child, we agonize to bring forth our immortal being from this chrysalis of animal limitation in which it is imprisoned. And, says St Paul, this is not the mere private struggle of each of us, it's the world's battle, it's what creation's for: the whole universe so far as we can know it is to find its sense and its glory in the freeing of our nature, in bringing the sons of God to the birth.

What is divine likeness? What is sonship to God? Jesus himself gives us the answer. It is an active openness of heart. Be ye therefore merciful (he says) as your Father is merciful. Give and forgive. That is the divine character. Our hearts are to be as open to love as our minds are open to truth.

Now if you think I am going to talk to you about practical generosity and Christian kindness, set your minds at rest. I wouldn't dare. You are Christians and you have the Spirit in your hearts. You are just as well qualified to preach to me as I to you on openness of heart. The only thing I can pretend to have that's at all extra is a specialist knowledge of the scripture, so let me show you a heavenly thing in this most heavenly gospel which we read today. It is about the mote in the eye. Anyone hearing this gospel can see this much, that Jesus is saying to us, 'Do not judge until you can see straight, do not offer yourself as a guide until you have cured your own blindness, do not try to teach others the spiritual lesson you have not learnt yourself.' So much is plain. But there's a very special point we are likely to miss, because it turns on Jewish ways of speech. When they talked about a good eye and a bad eye, they did not mean simply an eye that sees well and an eye that is misty or out of focus. For they had noticed how a mean man screws up his eyes when he is about to refuse a favour, and how a generous man opens his eye in welcome at your request, and smoothes the wrinkles round it. And so an unwrinkled eye, or a good eye, was a common phrase with them for a generous attitude. In fact, they would say 'a good eye' when we might say 'an open hand'.

What, then, is Jesus saying? He has been speaking, as we have seen, of that generosity which makes men like to God. Love, he says, do not judge; and especially, he says, do not dare to judge other men's generosity. How can you see the fault in their eye, unless your own eye is clear? No eye is clear that is not generous; and whose eye is generous, when he is judging another man to be mean?

The man who judges his neighbour screws up his eyes—he has a wicked eye, a blocked-up eye, and then, of course, he cannot see. The mean man screws up his eyes to shut his neighbour out, but in so doing he makes himself blind. All mean men are prejudiced: they see no more than they wish to see. They will not see what is there, in case it should cause them trouble, or put them to shame. Generosity sees, meanness is blind.

Now I want to go back from the end to the beginning. We said at the beginning that man's likeness to God is his capacity for the impartial eye and the open heart, and we talked as though these were two things. But now Jesus shows us that they are all one thing. For the closing of the heart screws up the eye, shuts out from us the vision of God and of man, imprisons us in our own dark narrow bodies. Only the generous eye can see out. If we have not the open heart of God, we have not the vision of the living truth, but (at the most) a dead assemblage of correct facts.

Jesus tells us more. He tells us that if we give and forgive, we shall receive great riches: good measure—shaken down, pressed together, and running over—will be poured into our laps. Now partly, I am sure, he is telling us that God will give to generous minds a heavenly reward; but is it not true in part that heaven begins here? The seeing eye, the loving heart, here and now, possesses all things. If a man who is not a Welshman says, 'Wales is my country', what does he mean? He was not born in it, he does not own an acre of it. It is his just by knowing and by appreciating it: it's his country because it's his delight, and it would make him no happier if he could put a fence round it, and lock the public out. Or if a man says, 'my poetry', 'my music', not meaning the verses he wrote, or the music he has in his record album; he means the poetry and the music in which he delights. They are his in a much more important sense through his delight in them, than in any physical possession he might have in them. Or if a good man talks of 'my dear people', how are they his, except by being dear? The open heart, and generous eye, do not wait for heaven to have their reward. Being one with the spirit of God, they possess all things. Satan pretends to us, just as he pretended to Jesus, that he can give us the riches of the world through greediness; but when Jesus had given himself away to us with both his hands, and suffered for us the death of the cross, then it was that he would say, 'All mastery is given to me in heaven and on earth.' That was, and is, the sovereignty of love, which Jesus won for us, and which he shares with us.

Based on the epistle and gospel for Trinity 4, Romans 8.18–23 and Luke 6.36–42.

Epstein's Lazarus

PREACHED IN NEW COLLEGE CHAPEL OXFORD

The dead came forth, tied hand and foot with grave-clothes.

JOHN 11.44

I have been reading an eloquent poem by A. L. Rowse upon your Lazarus over there. This makes me brave enough to preach about it, finding so sensitive a man in agreement with the interpretation of the work after which I had been groping myself. If I err, I shall err in good company. When I first saw the statue, I thought it was pretty queer: more gradually, I yielded to the spell, and should, perhaps, have understood quite readily if I had not been baffled by the local conditions. Lazarus is pulling himself together, bringing himself back with infinite pain from happy unconsciousness, or, let us say, from an unconsciousness neither happy nor unhappy, but welcomed as blessed relief in comparison with that painful borderland of the struggle for breath through which he had passed into not-being, and through which he must pass back from not-being into life once more. Can the life which calls him back be worth the passage through that nightmare of half-life which bars the way? If only Lazarus could be in both places at once—if his mind could run before his steps to feel the light and warmth of full existence, then he might be braced to endure the numbing cold of intervening twilight. But, especially in that state of almost-death, he is incapable to feel anything but what immediately confronts him, the cruel agony of reawaking. But why should I be selfish and not share with you the pleasure of Mr Rowse's poem? Hear what he has written:

> This is Lazarus: the head an egg
> Laid upon labouring shoulders,
> Or like a stone laid upon a cave.
> The clear Spring light gives life
> Making the cold stone breathe and move.
> Awake, O awake from the dream of death,
> After four days laid in the grave,
> The mumbled lips still shut, breath

Withheld, tongue seeking an outlet,
The eyes still sealed in sleep
Resisting awakening, the pain and grief
Of life, the body unfree, still bound
In the wound grave-clothes,
Arms pinioned, arrested in motion,
The body's life stirring in the wrapped
Limbs, now lapped and lipped in light
Passing a bird's wing over the stone erect.
Now a cloud sends Lazarus back to the dead;
And now the returning sun
Of Spring, of moving wings and flowers
Shooting from the earth-bound soil,
Of birds calling in the grove,
Calls him to awake and live.

This is Lazarus: this is he
Whom Jesus loved, over whom
He wept when they had laid him in the tomb
On the bitter road out of Bethany.
Now he has heard the word: see
The coffined breast bursting the bonds,
Leaning forward, urgent for life.
Not the life of stone intolerable to be borne
But the life of moving things,
Of growing flowers and birds' wings.
In the still chapel of the grave North
He begins to stir and move:
He has heard the Word:
'Lazarus, come forth!'

So, after all, the Word, the living Word of God, he who has also said, 'I am the light of the world', breaks through the twilight and reaches Lazarus: the word rings in his bandaged ears, the light filters through his closed eyelids. 'This is Lazarus,' says Mr Rowse, and he says it twice, but are we to believe him? Poets do not always mean what they say. Does Mr Rowse believe in Lazarus, the Lazarus of Bethany; or is what he sees in Lazarus some other reality for which Lazarus stands, and if so, what is it? And if poets do not always mean what they say, the governing bodies of colleges do not always plainly mean what they do. They have put Lazarus there, and you say at first sight, a traditional action; a figure of Lazarus the Christian saint is added to a Christian Chapel. But one does not see any of the apparatus of Christian cult, no candles, no encouragement to kneel and pray: he stands alone and coldly there. And then—most significant of all— this region of happy death from which he drags his eyes so unwillingly away—what is it? It appears to be the Warden, Fellows and Scholars of New College engaged in their devotions; it appears (even) to be the Chapel altar. What Lazarus is this? Is he not the typical New College man, tearing himself with agony and regret free from the sentimental falsehood of his school religion, the swaddling bands of pious lies, to confront the painful light of philosophic truth? And, when he has once got his head the right way round on his shoulders, when he has once cast the grave-clothes off, is not his next step going to be, to get out of the Chapel altogether by the west door which stands so conveniently before him? Is not the Chapel the sepulchre from which he is evoked, and is not the force evoking him (as Mr Rowse already appears to hint) the free daylight of the open air?

Who shall say, indeed, what the governing body meant, or what Mr Rowse meant, or (for that matter) what Jacob Epstein meant? To stick to Mr Rowse and Jacob Epstein, and to avoid speculation about that metaphysical entity, the corporate mind of a governing body—certainly no one writes a poem, no one cuts a statue, without identifying himself with the subject, and struggling alive with what then struggles into life. What struggle into life was Epstein expressing? Perhaps sculpture itself, the coming alive of stone under the sculptor's hands: Lazarus is just a statue, a statue coming to be; or he is the sculptor's thought being reborn out of the stone. And what is Mr Rowse expressing? What are life and light to him, and what the state of death? Every man, it seems, must experience his own Lazarus. Look at this Lazarus, he is your judgement; you must be Lazarus when you look at Lazarus, and know from what death you are returning, into what light of life you struggle to aspire.

You are Lazarus; and if you accept the position in which you are placed, the direction of the prevailing orientation, you are struggling out of the Chapel westwards in pursuit of the falling sun. For the sun of secular truth is falling: however sweet, however brilliant that light, it is the truth of a dying world. The

natural sciences set forth nature, and nature is dying, and philosophy expounds the universe of discourse, the laws of worldly
speech, which will have no currency when all our tongues are tied
in death. Look, Lazarus, back into the sanctuary towards the
east, struggle towards the light breaking from the altar, where
the Lamb of God lies slain, where from the cross and sepulchre of
Christ the light goes up which never will go down, but which
outshines the world: the light to which your painful eyes must
strain on that day of tearful rebirth.

> *Lacrymosa dies illa,*
> *Qua resurget ex favilla*
> *Judicandus homo reus*

when man in his guilt must arise from dust to judgement; and,
may it be, to mercy:

> *Huic ergo parce, Deus.*

That terrible light from beyond the world beats into the world and
afflicts us with the continual pain of resurrection. The light, says
St John in his first page, the light which was before the world shone
in the darkness of the world and the darkness comprehended it
not: moreover, in flesh and in person the light came into the world
to enlighten every man: but most men found the effort of rebirth
too much: the world acknowledged him not, his own received him
not. But as many as received him, they were reborn; to them
gave he the power to become the Sons of God. And so the light
travelling through the pages of St John's gospel, comes to rest full
upon the dark entry of Lazarus's tomb. Tears are shaken from the
eyes which are our everlasting day, and the Word of God which
first called light from darkness speaks: Lazarus, come forth.

The tears fall for us, the voice speaks to us, the struggle is for
us. You who come here to pray—I suppose you have come
here to pray, or for what have you come? What do you think that
prayer is? Go and look at Lazarus, and *be* Lazarus swaddled in
the deadness of a worldly mind, and finding that death sweet;
your head turned away backward, your eyes shut and blind, and
yet you cannot pull them away from their objects of no-vision, the
trivial amusement of the mind, the preoccupation with your own
vanity, to face the afflicting, the annihilating light of God. How
can you pray? It is nearly impossible to pray, but the overcoming

of that impossibility, that is just what prayer is. If you could pray when you set yourself to pray, then perhaps you would not need to pray. For perhaps it is right to say that the blessed Saints in heaven do not pray, they simply look upon the face of God and rejoice in the overflow of everlasting light. But you have got to pray—you have got to pray yourself out of prayerlessness. Do you care about the happiness of your friends? Very little. Do you care about their salvation? Not at all. Then must your prayers for them be insincere? Yes, they will be insincere while they are yours, for you are insincere, as insincere in your worldliness as you are insincere in your charity and faith. Nevertheless, pray in your insincerity, until your prayers cease to be yours alone, until the sun of God's charity has warmed you into life, and turned your heart of stone to a heart of flesh. You do not believe in God. No, but neither do you disbelieve. Your disbelief and your belief are insincere alike. Pray your insincere prayer until he who is sincerity and truth itself overcomes you, until his rays prise open your eyes, and you see that most blessed sight, a living love, a living will, a flame to cauterize your meanness and your frivolity, a light to sweeten every stale corner of your thought, a life better than your own in which to live. Go out and walk in that light—but the darkness will have you again, but you must pray again, be continually reborn. How dare you start the day in darkness, and not have prayed, or go in darkness and without prayer to rest?

You will come in and out of your chapel, and you will pass Lazarus, and you will say: 'I am Lazarus. I am dead, not alive. I cannot pray, therefore I come to pray.' You come to pray because, long before you thought of praying, the magnet had drawn your mind. There Lazarus agonizes, and he thinks it is all his work to will himself back from death into life. But none of us made himself, and none of us remakes himself, and death cannot achieve existence. If you are drawn to pray, it is because a word went forth, and a light shone, before the making of the world, and they reach as far as the heart of the world. What has God given you? The power to consent to omnipotent predestination; and not content with that, he woos your consent with sacrificial love. Now therefore to the word made flesh, and him crucified, be ascribed no less than to the Father and the Holy Ghost all might, dominion, majesty and power, henceforth and for ever.

Holy Angels

Fear not, for they that be with us are more than they that be with them.

2 KINGS 6.16

Do you ever read or hear the experiences of people who explore caves underground? Through the dark they go by the light of their torches, and then, maybe, they see a suspicion of light round the next bend of the tunnel they are following. They push on, and suddenly the roof goes up and up, and in the top there is a crack like a chimney. They cannot see through it, but that doesn't stop a long thin ray of light falling from it, and scattering itself in the vast cave, lighting up the dripping walls. Up at the top there are even a few ferns growing. Daylight! The explorers are suddenly reminded of the open-air world above. They think, if a mere trickle of sunlight can make the huge cave visible, what must be the power of the sun up there where he has free scope and nothing stands in his way? They remember the floods of golden glory pouring on land and sea, and looking at the pale green ferns in the roof, think of the flowers of every colour which drink life from sunlight in the fields and gardens of the world. What mugs we are, they may think, ever to have taken on this exploration down here in the dark.

Well now, there's a parable for you, and I dare say you've guessed the point of it already, knowing as you do the sort of groove that sermons follow. You'll have guessed that the cave in my story means the world, and that we ourselves are the explorers. We try to find our way about through this life by the light of our own torches, which are our natural wits and abilities; but then we meet traces of a light fully from above—the grace and the glory of God.

I wonder whether you have read the book by C. S. Lewis in which he describes his own early life, very much as a pilgrimage through a dark tunnel. He calls the book an odd name, *Surprised by Joy*—surprised by joy, because of the surprising gleams of glory that came down on his path from time to time, and which he traced at last to their origin, and found they came from God. So he became a Christian—he was an atheist before. If you and I began swapping stories about our own life, and especially our early life, no doubt we could tell one another about gleams of glory here and there, not only occasional glimpses of natural beauty that have taken our breath away. For instance, the sun going down over the sea and making a path of gold on the waves—not only glory like that, but occasional encounters with divine goodness in other men. Of all the luck I ever had, none was better than this—knowing a man who was, I believe, something of a saint; a man who did not *try* to love God, on and off, as you and I do, he just loved him, as young men love their wives or mothers their children, and he never thought about himself at all. Well, I tell about him freely to you, because he is dead, he threw his life away for his friends, as such men like to do. It is really stupid of me to talk to you about a man you didn't know but I do it to remind you of the gleams of glory you may yourselves have seen in the world of men.

Now those people in the cave, with whom I started—their thoughts ran up the ray of light as though it were a golden ladder, into the world above; and so I, remembering my friend now dead, may run up in thought to the God who made him, and whose glory he reflected. For God has made every one of us in his own image, after his own likeness, even though, alas, the eyes of God do not look out through our eyes as they look out through the eyes of the saints. But when I think of this man, who was my friend, it is easy for me to see the ray of glory there, and to trace it up to God.

Why the glory of God shines so dimly in this world of men, is a question we might discuss for a great while. Some of us know well enough why his glory shines so faintly on our own faces, because we each of us know our own vices. But we will not talk of that now. Let's take it for granted that this world is a strange mixture of the bright and the dark, as St John says on the first page of his gospel, 'The Light shineth in the darkness, and the darkness comprehended it not.'

Here the light shines in darkness, a ray through the roof of our cave; but somewhere above, the Light shines in Light, and fills a world of Light. Somewhere above, the goodness of God just overflows like water from a fountain and meets no obstacle. There, all his creating, making power pours out in splendid creatures, unspoilt beings, worthy of the God who makes them: they, like God himself, are light, and in them is no darkness at all. We call them the holy angels.

Why do we believe in the holy angels? What's the point of it? Well, obviously we believe in them on the word of Jesus Christ, on the testimony of saints and of the holy Church, and because it was an angel brought the tidings to Mary when she conceived by the Holy Ghost. But if you ask what is the principal part of the belief—why we are to suppose that God created angels—I shall reply that the puzzle isn't why God created angels, but why he ever created anything else. It does not puzzle me, that the sun in the sky surrounds himself with light, for it's his nature to shine in all directions; so why should it puzzle me that God surrounds himself with glorious angels, in whom his creative goodness is displayed? The sun shoots the same quality of light in all directions, up, down and round, but on this point the sun differs from God, who never sends out two rays of glory which are alike. His power is so various, that each of his creatures expresses it differently: Michael, Gabriel, Raphael, thousands on thousands of shining spirits, each serve and love God in their own unique way and reflect a different aspect of his infinite glory.

Why do we believe in angels? We start from what we can see, the glory of God in this mixed world of bright and dark. We say, this world of ours isn't the home of glory, glory comes from above; it descends, as St James says, from the Father of lights, in whom is no change nor shadow of alteration. We trace glory up to its home, and ask, how that home is furnished and populated? We reply, it is peopled with angels.

When the enemies of Jesus came to take him at Gethsemane, when Judas kissed him, when Peter drew his sword, 'Put back thy sword again into its sheath,' said Jesus. 'Thinkest thou I could not, if I wished, entreat my Father, and he send me even now more than twelve regiments of angels?' When Jesus used these words, Peter understood exactly what he meant, for Peter, like any Jewish child, knew the story of Elisha; the story to which, in speaking thus, Jesus was plainly alluding. For Elisha, once, had been looked for by armed enemies, as Jesus then was; and Elisha's disciple had been as troubled as were the disciples of Jesus in Gethsemane, when he saw the flash of swords. 'Alas, my master', said he, 'what are we to do?' 'Fear not', said Elisha, 'for they that be with us are more than they that be with them.' Then Elisha prayed, and said, 'Lord, I pray thee, open his eyes, that he may see.' So (we read) the Lord opened the eyes of the young man, and he saw; and behold the mountain was full of horses and chariots of fire round about Elisha. These were the hosts of God, these were the holy angels made for the moment visible to that disciple's mind, so he might understand what Elisha had told him: they that be with us are more than they that be with them.

They that be with us are more than they that be with them: the forces of God, the allies of the Church, far out-balance the enemies of the Church, the forces of Satan; even though it doesn't look like it to our beclouded eyes. How weak, how few we are! and how much we're up against! How much you are up against, in the parishes where your homes are. You're a mere handful, aren't you, compared with the masses of indifference and unbelief. Well, but remember, we only see what's in the cave, and if we get into rocket-ships and go whizzing to the moon or even as far as Mars, we shall still only be flitting about like bats inside the great cave of the world. The heaven of angels is God's open air, and it is far greater than the world of men. The forces of God are overwhelmingly strong, the balance of power in his creation is all on the diviner side; and how could it be otherwise, since God is God? They that are for us are more, many, many times more, than they that are against us. We see a contrast between the disciple of Elisha in the Old Testament, and the disciples of Jesus in the New. Elisha's disciple saw the regiments of angels, standing by to rescue his master; and they did rescue him. The disciples of Jesus did not see any twelve legions of angels, for their divine master refused to summon them: he would not be rescued, he went to his death. Yet by that very death Jesus opened the eyes of his disciples to see the angels, for whom in his greatest need he had refused to pray. The women went to his sepulchre on the third day, and there the angels were, one at the head, one at the feet, of the place where Jesus had lain. It was by dying that Jesus set open for ever a door between earth and heaven: his sepulchre is a piece of heaven, a place of angels. Where Jesus lies sacrificed for us, heaven is opened, a great shaft of light falls from above, and the angels of God are seen ascending and descending upon the Son of Man.

For the act of love which makes the Son of God die for us brings all the angels down. Those pure spirits, those brave and flaming hearts have been loving the Lord their God ever since they were created, with all their mind and soul and strength: but they have never been able to make him such an offering as they see Jesus make, when he gives himself to die for us men and for our salvation. So the air is thick with wings, wherever a Christian priest, by Christ's command, brings back upon the altar the sacrifice of Christ; and whenever we offer the Holy Sacrament we are bidden to join our weak praises with the whole choir and company of heaven, with angels and archangels lauding and magnifying the only Glorious Name, and crying Holy, Holy, to him with whose glory heaven and earth are filled.

See, then, with whom we unite, and whose supplicating voices support our prayers here: certainly when we gather before the altar we know that they who are with us are more than they who are with our enemies.

One Sunday it happened that St John could not be at church with his friends, for like Elisha, like Jesus, he was taken by the armed men, and held in prison. But God consoled him with a vision: he saw the Christian sacrament that morning not as men see it, but as it is seen in heaven. His spirit went up; he saw the throne of Glory, and the four cherubim full of eyes in every part, who sleep not, saying Holy, Holy, Holy. And he saw the sacrifice, the Lamb of God: a Lamb standing as though slaughtered; a Lamb alone worthy to open for mankind the blessed promises of God. He saw the Lamb, and then the angels. I saw, he says, and heard the voice of many angels round about the Throne, the number of them ten thousand times ten thousand, and thousands of thousands: saying with a loud voice, Worthy is the Lamb who was slain to receive the power and riches and wisdom and might and honour and glory and blessing.

That is the Christian Eucharist. Certainly when we gather here, those that are with us are more than those who stand upon the opposing side. For all heaven is one with us, when once we lift our hearts up to the Lord, and praise the everlasting Love, the One God in three Persons, Father, Son, and Holy Ghost; to whom be ascribed, as is most justly due, all might, dominion, majesty and power, henceforth and for ever.

Also preached in Holy Angels, Cranford, Middx (1955); St James's, Piccadilly, London (1962); and St Michael's, Abingdon, Berks (1963).

A New Creation

PREACHED IN KEBLE COLLEGE CHAPEL 1965

> Hail the day that sees him rise
> Glorious to his native skies

So sings Charles Wesley—or perhaps not Charles Wesley, but Thomas Cotterill, credited with having altered the words in the year of our Lord 1820. But never mind which of them it was, since neither of them is going to answer my rhetorical question. My dear Charles—or ought I to say, my dear Thomas—what do you mean? You seem to be saying the same sort of thing as:

> See the canny Scot return
> To his native Bannockburn

Only that the glorious person of whom you speak had his birth-place somewhere among the celestial galaxies, not in the less habitable half of this island. Well, since—my dear Thomas, or should I say, Charles—you are not in a position to answer me, I must try to play your hand for you out of dummy. And I feel pretty confident that you would reply that I am interpreting you too literally. For, you would say, when Christ returned into his native and celestial glory, it was the divine life of the Son of God that so returned, since as for the human life of Jesus, the birth-place from which it entered on its course was at Bethlehem, not in the skies at all. And to call the skies, or any other place, the birthplace of the Son of God must be taken to be a figure of speech, for the 'mysterious begetting' of the Son of God does not have a time, still less a place: it is a timeless dimension of social love within the beginning of the Godhead.

Besides (our orthodox and learned hymnographer continues) our scriptural warrant for what we say is in St John's Gospel, in the prayers of Christ: 'And now, O Father, glorify me beside thee with the glory I had beside thee ere ever the world was.' Evidently the skies are not the native place of the divine Son, for he was with his Father when there were as yet no skies for him to inhabit. So much, I think, the very orthodox hymn-writer must be bound to say. But at the next step in the discussion I lose all confidence in my power to ventriloquize an answer on his behalf. This is when he is called on to face the obvious question: 'Then what makes you say "native skies?" You say it's a figure of speech; well, lying has been called a figure of speech. Why use a figure of speech which is 100 per cent misleading?' I do not know what our hymn-writer would say to this. We must do the best we can for ourselves. What shall we say? I should say that the force of the figure is that of a simple comparison. We are virtually confined to this planet; and even the Americans and Russians to the solar system. Outside lies the unimaginable spread of astral space, which constantly radiates upon us, and out of which, perhaps, aeons ago, our little system was somehow blown together. Well now, put the whole universe of galaxies in the place of our little world, and say the following formula: 'As our little world is cradled in outer space, so is the universe cradled in God's immensity.' Or, to put it otherwise, 'the universe is the sky of our little world: God's immensity is, as it were, the sky of the universe.' Such is the figure of speech, for what it is worth; but I am not sure that Dame Julian of Norwich was not better inspired, when she saw the universe as a very small thing, like a nut, lying in the palm of God's hand.

But Dame Julian is not our present business; let us return to Wesley's hymn. 'Hail the day that sees him rise/Glorious to his native skies.' He says 'rise' you will notice, not 'return', and that is not, I think, simply for the sake of the rhyme. For the marvel is not that the celestial Son of God returns where he belongs, but that the earthborn Jesus rises into the native heaven of that divine life which had become man in him. The manhood he has taken, he does not relinquish: 'Though returning to the Throne/Still he calls mankind his own.' He is not the man of flesh and blood which each of us now is, but he is the man glorified, which each of us may hope by his grace to become. And what we shall be in glory, we do not know, except that we shall be most fully ourselves, through being full of God.

So, then, the dear man who lived and died for us is gone beyond the limits and the confines of this world into the immensity of God. But that does not mean that he is merged and lost in the placeless life of Godhead, like a drop of water in the ocean. It means that there is a new creation, a new world beyond this world, a world not of flesh and blood, nor a world of interlocking physical energies, but a world of which the substance, not yet known to us, is the new-minting of God's hand, a world of Christhood, of glorified human nature, of Jesus, and of all those united with Jesus, and, through him, united with the life of God.

It is the obvious meaning of the Ascension faith that Jesus is in some sense taken out of the world—not so that he might be made distant from us, but so that he might be freed from the limitations of physical being and new-minted in the image of the Glory of God. And so there are two worlds: our universe, the place of God's natural creatures; Christ's heaven, the place of God's glorified creatures. In either world God is everywhere present by his power and his grace; but more fully in that other world where the hearts of the redeemed offer no obstacles to his invisible action, and most fully in the glorious man, Jesus Christ, whom he has made personally one with his divine life. The mind of God speaks from his lips to the citizens of that country; they see the love of God in the kindness of his eyes.

There are two worlds, then; and if we do not call that other world 'heaven', then what are we to call it? Those theologians who say that 'heaven' is an image which means nothing to our age had better be careful what they say. To localize infinite God in heaven, or anywhere else, is a gross metaphysical error; in this or in any other age. But if there is not a society of persons in bliss, new-created and centred on a glorified Jesus, then our Christ is nothing but a dead Jew and to talk of Christianity is sentimental folly. But we know a living Christ, and we know he is not unaccompanied; and what shall we call that company, but heaven?

There are two worlds, the old and the new creations of God; but if they are two, then how are they related to one another? Surely the answer of our faith is plain. Our world does not contain Christ's, but Christ's world embraces ours. Since Christ's world is not physical, it is no part of our universe: for our universe is nothing but an interaction of energies, a tissue of dynamic space, and what is not physical has no place in it. No lines of radiation which any telescope can follow will reach it, no curvature of light will show the pull of its influence. But our world is in Christ's heaven: for that is a world where spirit touches spirit. Those heavenly minds can know whatever minds are opened to them by God's will and permission: so we are present to Christ; and so he inflows upon us.

There is no way from here into heaven, while this life lasts; but all heaven adopts us. And so faith strikes boldly at the heart of heaven, and starts with the Christ who makes us his. To lift up our hearts, and put them with the Lord, is the beginning of our eucharistic action: and so it is of all Christian prayer. We have just to remember that we are in his world, known, yes and loved through and through, by the man in whom is the Godhead: and then to form our prayers as the extension of his thoughts.

'It is expedient for you', said Jesus in St John, 'that I depart from you.' Expedient! expedient that he should so place himself that he might furnish a living line of love from every believer's heart to the heart of God. Expedient—but will it seem expedient, when on the day of judgement we are made to see what treasures of grace have been poured before us, and how our neglect of them condemns us? But it will be expedient, since he also died for us. We will take refuge with the precious blood.

Pearls of Great Price

PREACHED IN TRINITY COLLEGE CHAPEL OXFORD 1957

The kingdom of heaven is like unto a man that is a merchant seeking goodly pearls; and having found one pearl of great price, he went and sold all that he had, and bought it. MATT. 13.45–6

This is not really a sermon, but a tutorial discussion broken loose. We all know that tutors must not preach at their pupils. But they must be allowed their compensations. The sermon suppressed in the study may be permitted to break out in full spate across the Chapel floor.

But for a start we will go back to the study. My pupil has been explaining to me his views on a very well-worn philosophical text. The old philosopher is trying to make out a case for the superior pleasantness of a virtuous life. Cads, the philosopher has to admit, often seem to have a glorious time; but, he says, only seem to. Their pleasures are more apparent than real. The commentators (whom my pupil is also acquainted with, in a distant sort of way) join in a howl of derision. Nonsense, they say, pleasures lie in seeming: they are as real as they feel. If cads feel pleased over their caddish delights, then they *are* pleased. It is nonsense to call any felt pleasure false.

But my pupil for once (and how rarely this happens!) disagrees with the commentators and champions the ancient sage. 'What these people say', he remarks, 'may be all very well in theory, but I'm sure Plato is on to something. What he's talking about—well, it's what happens when you get a bit drunk. First of all you think you are having a marvellous time. But after a bit, you see you weren't, really; it was all a fraud.' 'Well,' I say, 'but what was a fraud? You felt jolly, didn't you, while it lasted? That wasn't a fraud. And the drink went down nicely: that wasn't a fraud, either.' 'No, that wasn't the fraud,' says my pupil, 'but there was a fraud, all the same. The fraud was, I thought I was absolutely at the top of my form, and making marvellous jokes. But looking at it afterwards, I see that I wasn't exercising the mastery of wit I thought I was, I was being pretty feeble. So my being pleased with myself was a take-in. And I'll tell you another take-in,' he continues. 'I thought I was getting to know one or two of the other characters at the party wonderfully well and better than ever before. But after the event, I can see I wasn't really. We weren't getting to know anything: we were just getting warmed-up together.' 'I dare say you're right,' I say, 'and of course it isn't my line to recommend insobriety as the path to mutual acquaintance. All the same, you wouldn't say, would you, that getting warmed-up never leads to any genuine discoveries? Take falling in love. What's so fantastic about it is, that all the commonplace trash in the poets is perfectly true. When you're in that state of mind, you see everything with amazing vividness: the violets look twice as blue and the song of the thrushes is ten times as sweet. And what you see in the girl—well, she's just a girl, admittedly, but God made her, and there's an awful lot in her to see, as there is in all his works; and if for once you can see some of what's there to see, surely that's nothing to complain of; that's not a fraud, is it?'

My pupil views me with compassion: dear, dear, the romanticism of these middle-aged men! 'No, but there is a fraud,' he says. 'You think the girl's IT, and of course she isn't.' No; and so, for all there may be in her, she is to be dropped, is she, as an impostor, who had falsely pretended to be IT? Like a merchant man, seeking goodly pearls, who found one pearl of great price and went and sold all that he had, and bought it. For this was it, the truly perfect pearl. What is IT; that which is no fraud, so that we can never wake up sober and say, I thought that was it, but of course it wasn't, really.

Now, perhaps, we can appreciate the meaning of St Peter's declaration, recorded for us in the second lesson. What do men say that Jesus is? Some say this, others say that. But what do his disciples say? St Peter speaks for them: 'Thou art the Christ.' You can seek a learned answer to what the fable meant, by searching the Old Testament, and later Jewish books. But for a practical answer, 'You are IT' might do. St Peter has found what will never be a fraud. To work with Messiah is to do what you are for, and to help achieve what the world is for. And the pearl of great price, once found, is always in our pockets, or rather, in our hearts—we have only to put our hands into our bosoms, to find it there. For there are always Christ's commands to be obeyed; there is always

Christ in heaven, so that we can any time lift up our minds, remember him, and share his living thoughts; there is always Christ to be sought next morning in his sacrament. We need never be put off with frauds: we can always be having, and doing, what we are for. This is IT.

After the drinking-party, there is the morning of cold reflection, which remorselessly peels the false colours off the previous night's glories; and there are many such inevitable hours in life, the sobering ends to cheerful periods for instance when a man gets a bad, or no, degree, and reassesses the value of his career as an undergraduate bridge-player. Our last hour on earth might seem to provide the most searching of all soberings-up. Only then, with the aid of medical skill and medical mendacity, we may hope to skip the consciousness of it, and sink into eternity on cushions of morphia. But no, this is too good to be true, justice cannot be cheated so, there is a day of reckoning.

> Seated high, the Judge will reign;
> All that's hidden will be plain
> And no unrighted wrongs remain.

In former times what struck men about the Day of Judgement was that it would forbid men to get away with their crimes, but what may strike us about it, is that it will make us acknowledge our follies. Then we shall see face to face that supreme Good, which day by day and year by year we have neglected for toys and trifles. And the more we read in his eyes the light of mercy, the more grounds we shall have to condemn our own perversity, for having turned our backs day by day, and hour by hour, on so kind a Creator.

St Peter himself has a black crime to confess in that presence— he denied his master; yet nothing can alter the fact that he devoted his life to the service of Christ, braved persecution and incurred martyrdom. But we, who live a more mixed and ordinary life, and have made no visible heroic sacrifice—how will it be for us? It is not that the Christ of God cannot be sought and found and served in an ordinary life. It is that we shall have to consider in what proportion of our life we have remembered the pearl which God has placed in our bosoms. That will be our Day of Judgement.

> What advocate can I command,
> What plea, alas, shall take in hand
> When the righteous hardly stand?

The Christian poet who describes the Last Day appeals to his judge:

> O King of fear and majesty,
> Saving whom thou savest, free,
> Fount of pity, pity me.
>
> Thou soughtest me with toil and pain,
> Thou hungest on the tree to gain
> My pardon; surely not in vain.

'Thou soughtest me'—the kingdom of heaven is like unto a man that is a merchant seeking goodly pearls, who, when he had found one pearl of great price . . . Why, what have we been saying? Have we not, in our unconscious egotism, been reading Christ's parable the wrong way round? We have been comparing the kingdom of heaven to the pearl of price, and ourselves, or the heroes among us, to the merchant man. And yet that is not what Christ says. The kingdom of heaven, he says, is like a merchant man—and when Christ says 'the kingdom of heaven', as often as not he means 'the Royal Majesty of God' or, more simply, 'the Divine King'. God the King, then, is like a merchant man. But if so, what is the pearl? Look at the other parables with which the evangelist aligns this, and you will see. God is a peasant, who wants a crop, and he does not mind how much of the seed miscarries, as long as there is a harvest. God is a fisherman, who wants a catch: he does not mind how much rubbish comes in the net, as long as there are fish worth picking out. He is a shepherd, who will leave his flock to fend for itself, while he drags after the one lost sheep. He is a merchant man, who has set his heart on one pearl of great price, and thinks everything well lost, to gain it. So what is the pearl of price?

> Remember, Lord, thy arduous way
> In quest of me, and hear me pray:
> Lose not the found, on judgement day.
>
> Thou soughtest me with toil and pain,
> Thou hungest on the tree to gain
> My pardon; surely not in vain.*

* From the *Dies Irae* by Thomas of Celano, now used as part of the Mass for the Dead. This translation is Farrer's own version, designed to be chanted.

You are the pearl of price. A loyal and obedient heart is what the King of Heaven thinks the world well lost to win, and since he puts such a price on our souls, he has the best right to bid us not to undervalue them. He who will buy Peter with his precious blood is he who says to Peter: 'What shall it profit a man to gain the whole world, and lose his soul? Or what shall he trade in exchange for his soul?'

The parable of the pearl, then, describes the King of Heaven's quest for us, not our quest for him. And yet it is not perverse to take it the other way round as well. For we cannot go wrong, to imitate God. And if he sets an infinite value on the image of his face where it is shaped in us in mortal clay, we cannot go wrong, to value it in its heavenly original, or to love that Son, in whom the Father's heart supremely delights.

But though there is a two-way traffic, the King of Heaven seeking us, we seeking him, no one can doubt which of these searches is the more effective for our salvation. He has set his heart on us, and this is the best hope any of us can entertain: that our setting of our hearts on him is sufficient to make the bond between us a reality, so that he may draw us to himself, and in that other world pull us through the fire that purges us, and burn our rubbish away.

There result from what we have been saying two very simple truths. God is priceless to us, for what he is makes him so. We are priceless to God, for his kindness makes us so. Why then should I remember God, and serve God, day and night? Because he is all that is worth having to me; and because I am infinitely desired by his love. It needed no Christ to teach us that God is our sole and everlasting Good could we but attain him: what Christ showed us was that God desires us with all the love of his infinite heart.

Giving and Receiving

PREACHED IN KEBLE COLLEGE CHAPEL OXFORD 1964

There was a scientific exhibition a few years ago, in which a computer was exhibited which had been taught to play infallible chess. However, my friend Dr Mascall, an ingenious mathematician, took it on. He played some highly unorthodox moves, and foxed the machine completely. Dr Mascall won; and this was a great consolation to those of us who like to think that we are still cleverer than machines. Even more recently a computer was taught to measure the style of different writers. This time it was St Paul who floored the machine. For the machine decided that the authentic Paul, who wrote Romans and Corinthians and Galatians, didn't write Philippians. But that's plain silly. Philippians is the most intensely personal of all his letters. There was no point in anyone's forging it, for it grinds no axe, it teaches no special doctrine. It is just a conversation with friends about matters of common interest and no forger known to us from the ancient world comes near to having the skill to have invented it, specially not the last chapter. The people at Philippi had sent him a present of money, and the Apostle, who liked to keep himself by his own manual labour, quite falls over his feet in trying to say in one breath that he is immensely grateful and that he could do just as well without it. Whatever he may say, we can see that he was deeply touched: he overflows with happiness and affection, at being so kindly remembered by his friends. He gives them the news, of course, and the news isn't really very good. For the fact is, he is probably going to be killed before he can see them, but he makes the best of it. If God wants him to live on, and be a bit more use to the Philippians, God will see to it. If he dies, it will be because it is best. It will be his contribution to the sacrifice we have all to make in union with Christ's death, and as for himself, he will be with Christ—and what could be better?

Since St Paul wears his heart on his sleeve, perhaps it is no impertinence on our part to say that pride was his besetting temptation. Of course his pride was not of the childish sort which is out for status and outward dignity. That sort of pride would not have led him to stitch tents in Aquila's shop, rather than draw an apostle's salary. No, his pride was of an altogether subtler sort; he would rather give than receive. He saw himself as a sort of universal father, providing for his spiritual children. And of course it was true: that's what he was. And at the same time he did learn to take. He saw that he couldn't carry on his mission without his disciples' friendship and prayers. And when he was old, and helpless, and in prison, it was his friends' turn to give, and his to receive. It was all one life they had together in Christ: now it flowed this way, now it flowed that way; whichever way the current of giving went, it was a common happiness.

I am specially struck by St Paul's grace in taking, because I had a friend in College with me who had very much the same sort of character but even more onesidedly. He was a clever, competent man, and a most generous one. He wanted to do everything for everybody. He ended up as head of an institution which he ran better than anyone had run it before; he was everyone's wise uncle and cared for everyone's worries. He overdid it, and fell ill. All he needed was a year's rest. But he couldn't be dependent, he couldn't bear to take: so what did he do? He went and killed himself. No doubt his mind was unhinged, none of us thought of blaming him. But if he had learned to take as well as to give, I do not think his illness would have led to so tragic a conclusion.

Pride is everyone's temptation, and especially the temptation of the male sex: and in the male sex, especially of the younger half. You indeed are not worried, like St Paul, about taking money—if you were, you would all be pitching yourselves over the parapet of Magdalen Tower. Nor, perhaps, at being catered for by services of various kinds, of which we are all more quick to detect the faults than to decline the benefits. No: but you like to be indebted to no one for the thing you make of your life. It seems a humdrum sort of achievement to follow a course of study proposed by the syllabus, or to master a reading-list supplied by your tutor. Each of you hopes in his secret heart to break out in some entirely new direction, to start a university newspaper quite unlike any other newspaper, to found or at least run a society—or, of course, easiest of all, to cover yourself with glory on the athletic field. If I were to believe the testimonials written about you (which,

needless to say, I do not) I should have to conclude that the
College is full of leaders with no one for them to lead. If we
could bring back dear Mr Keble from the grave to read through
testimonials, I think he would be puzzled. He would wipe his
spectacles, and give half a glint of a smile, and say, 'Dear me!
What is all this about *leadership*? I have always supposed the
virtue of a student to be *docility*.'

Docility means just teachableness. Of course, it has become a
bad word: we speak of 'docile sheep'. It suggests a *de haut en bas*
relationship, and would put your tutors in a position which would
embarrass them greatly. I would suggest to you instead the idea of
appreciativeness, of willingness to take. What a tutor, or a college
chaplain, or any such person really wants is to be eaten up alive.
He does not want to be believed, any more than argued with. He
wants to be drawn out, and devoured.

And so, of course, in your relations with one another. You
all want to impress your friends; all right, but let them impress
you. It's only fair. So far, the advice does not go beyond worldly
wisdom. But think that in every man you have the unique handiwork of God, and remember that it is the appreciative, not the
grudging, eye that sees what's there.

And indeed, now I have called up the saintly shade of Mr Keble,
I feel kind of uncomfortable about the worldly way this sermon is
going. Why do we take so long coming to the point? Pride sterilises
human relations, true enough. But that's not the worst of it: it's
death to the soul. So far as men are concerned, it's true that in the
end I have to make my own life. I may open myself to mankind,
but no friend, no teacher, no human idol is to lead me. But God
—no, God himself does not want to keep me in infantile leading-
strings, either. It will be enough if I open myself to admire what
deserves admiration, to love what is worthy of love, and to learn
what most repays attention. To think that a preoccupation with
my own clever pursuits, or the scoring of my own little successes,
should ever close my eyes to the work God works in the whole
fabric of this world, and in my neighbour, and in myself! The
more I see of the wisdom of his work, and of the depth of his love,
the more, not less, will be the calls on my powers of origination or
contrivance. In a vacuum of emptiness our manly freedom would
go for nothing. God is the very world of opportunity to his saints.

He so enriches their environment by his manifold presence, they have more than enough to do, now and to all eternity.

Let us hope that our worship here together, and our life here in common, may be a constant opening of the heart to God and to one another, in union with Jesus Christ, the only perfect lover of God, and lover of men: because he is bone of our bone, and flesh of our flesh, and because, being of one Godhead with the Father, he has heart enough to love all that the infinite heart is able to give.

On Being an Anglican

PREACHED IN PUSEY HOUSE OXFORD 1960

You know those correspondences they have in *The Times*. A reader in East Sussex has heard the cuckoo. This stimulates a reader in Cheshire to raise a question about the reason for calling cuckoo-flowers cuckoo-flowers; and a Lancashire reader rejoins with an attack on the teaching of botany in schools. I can't remember where this month's correspondence started from— perhaps it began with the decline of bird-watching among the rural clergy, but anyhow they have got round to discussing the bankruptcy of the parochial system. And now, in comes a man with a grievance—'My conviction', he says, 'that the parochial system is finished, and my loss of confidence in the official Church leadership, led me to renounce my Orders several years ago.'

My interest in the *Times* correspondence is seldom strong enough to compete with the attractions of toast and coffee, but I own that when I got as far as this my consumption slacked off. Here was an extraordinary man. There was nothing indeed surprising in a priest's becoming discouraged by the ineffectiveness of his parochial ministry, or by the spectacle of an equal lack of success in neighbouring parishes; nothing surprising in his finding it the last straw that the diocesan bosses should be content to run the show as it was and remain innocent of any concern for radical reorganization. What I found staggering was, that a man should allege these simple facts, and then, with an apparent confidence in general approval, go on to tell the world: 'So I renounced my Orders.' It would be about as consequent to say: 'He called me a Scotsman, so I shot him through the head'; and expect the judge and jury to dismiss you without a stain on your character.

Or would it? Perhaps it all depends on the point of view. Suppose our letter-writer regards the Church of England as a propaganda society founded by Henry VIII for inducing the subjects of the crown to attend public worship. He was himself a paid official of the society. But finding that the propaganda-machine didn't work, and that the head executives were bankrupt of ideas for making it work, he very naturally resigned his job. It was the conscientious (as well as, perhaps, the prudent) thing to do.

Yes, I know. But the reason why I find the ex-parson's letter so staggering is that it implies his holding this view of the Church, and how could he? It is true that we use such phrases as 'the ministry of the Church of England', 'a C. of E. parson'. Such phrases have their use. But fundamentally we are just Christian priests, priests in the Church of God. Did not Christ establish sacraments, and an apostolic ministry, and a visible company of faithful men? And have we not to make the best we can of it, by the grace of God? Are there too many ministers to give the sacraments to the Christians we have? Or are the sacraments to cease because the ministers find the ecclesiastical organization antiquated and suppose their bishops to be unimaginative? *A* is a layman and *B* is a laywoman, *C* is a priest and *D* is a nun: each, in the vocation wherewith he is called, goes to make the body of Christ; and between them the whole multitude of Christians must do the best they can, by the grace of God. Suppose the organization *is* antiquated, the leadership weak; we shall not help to modernize the former or invigorate the latter, by deserting our stations.

Well, but polity is more than party; a man dissatisfied with the Socialist machine, the Socialist ideology, may become a Liberal instead. The Church of England is only one among many organized Christian groups. To call it '*the* Church' is just social arrogance. It is the Church by law established, whatever that may mean; but in practice it has lost the privileges and retained the inconveniences of legal status. If I judge some other machine more effective than the Anglican for christianizing England, should I not transfer my allegiance?

No, for the political parallel is misleading. The true end of political action is to promote the prosperity, contentment and decent life of the citizens. The possession of these blessings is quite independent of membership of any political party. But the work of the Church is to incorporate men in the life of Incarnate God, and the Church is itself the means and the form of such an incorporation. We do not have our worldly happiness in the Socialist party, but we have our membership of Christ in the Church. So in the Church we must abide.

But look, you will protest, there you go again: 'In the Church'. There are many Churches; what business have you to call the Church of England *the* Church? It is time we grasped the nettle of the question. The Church of England is not *the* Church; there is only one Church, as there is only one Christ. The centre of the Church is neither Rome nor Canterbury; it is the heart of Heaven. There is a company of saints who enjoy the society of Jesus Christ more intimately than his disciples ever did on earth. We, who only know him by faith and touch him only in sacraments, are no more than outposts and colonies of his sacred empire. The fatherland is above, and there the vast body of the citizens reside. How many in heaven, and on earth, how few!

And even these few, how scattered, how divided! The everlasting shepherd promised that his flock should be one fold: and so it will at last in the heavenly Jerusalem. But as for earthly unity, in the present state of our warfare, it is a promise which, like other divine promises, depends on human obedience for its full effect. God has promised us salvation, and pledged it to us with his sacred blood. Yet he has warned us that where many are called, few may be chosen. He has promised us unity, and made his death the bond; but our perversity has made schisms and heresies. The Church feels herself to be one, and groans to find herself divided, but there is no easy way to heal all her divisions.

Meanwhile, how can I, truly and with a good conscience, abide in the Church of God? Only by remaining in the Church of England. But why? Because the people there are visibly the most pious, or the missionary action visibly the most efficacious, the ceremonies the most dignified or the most congenial? No. It is not for me to admire or embrace, or even prefer, a sect called Anglicanism. What is it then? There are two overriding considerations. I dare not dissociate myself from the apostolic ministry, and the continuous sacramental life of the Church extending unbroken from the first days until now. That is the first point, and the second is this: I dare not profess belief in the great Papal error. Christ did not found a Papacy. No such institution appeared for several hundred years. Its infallibilist claim is a blasphemy, and never has been accepted by the oriental part of Christendom. Its authority has been employed to establish as dogmas of faith, propositions utterly lacking in historical foundation. Nor is this an old or faded scandal—the papal fact-factory has been going full blast in our own time, manufacturing sacred history after the event.

I cannot desert the apostolic ministry, I cannot submit to the Pope. And I was not born a Greek or Slavic Christian. I was born in this English-speaking world, where God's merciful providence has preserved the form and substance of the Catholic Church, and freed it from papal usurpation. At first, the Church, liberated from the Pope, fell heavily under the hand of the king, but the bondage was not lasting. That royalism is an accident to our faith, is made evident by the healthy condition of the American Episcopal Church, where prayers are not offered for Queen Elizabeth. The Crown is no part of our religion. Not that this need prevent us from wishing most fervently that God may save our royal house, to be the happy and unquestioned centre of our loyal affection, or the source of humane and Christian influences in the state. While we worship a King above, our vision will be assisted by the shadow of a throne below, and the very criticism which strips the unrealities of regal state, may discover to us the true pattern of sovereignty in him who made us.

When reunion is discussed, it is a sentiment as inevitable as it is amiable on diplomatic lips, to say that all Churches have their peculiar riches; that we disvalue no one's treasures by prizing our own, but hope that everything of worth may find its place in the final synthesis. Such sentiments are wholesome, if they lead us to look for merits rather than defects in other denominations. But the effect is less wholesome if we are led by such talk to suppose that Anglicanism should be valued as a charming or quaint or rare or beautiful species of ecclesiastical plant. We have our saints, some fostered by the Anglican spirit, some in revolt against it. But saints belong to Christendom: our saints are not ours. And though various edifying traditions of piety, learning and social action have flourished among us, they might perhaps as well have flourished somewhere else. It will be a sad admission, if our tree has produced no flowers or fruits—an admission we are happily not obliged to make. But we are not Anglicans because of these; because of George Herbert, or Dr Donne, or Isaac Walton, or Bishop Ken, or John Wesley, or John Keble—because of Prayer-Book English, or Cathedral psalmody, or Cambridge theology, or Oxford piety. No, we are Anglicans because we can obey Christ in this Church, by abiding in the stock and root of his planting, and in the sacramental life. We may begin by making a fuss about the Church, as a clever boy may make a fuss about a telescope, admiring its mechanism of tubes and lenses, and fiddling with the gadgets. But the purpose of the telescope is to eliminate itself and leave us face to face with the object of vision. So long as you are aware of the telescope you do not see the planet. But look, suddenly the focus is perfect; there is the hard ball of silver light, there are the sloping vaporous rings, and there the clear points, the satellites. And where is the telescope? It is no more to us than the window-pane through which we look into our garden.

The Church mediates Christ: her sacraments make Christ present, her creed presents the lineaments of his face, her fellowship incorporates us in his body. To be a loyal churchman is hobbyism or prejudice, unless it is the way to be a loyal Christian. Christ is our calling, Christ our life; he whom the cross could not daunt nor the grave retain will make our dry bones live, and restore to the universal Church that peace and unity that are agreeable to his will, that we may be one in him, as he with the Father and the Holy Ghost is one life, one love, one God.

Reaping Faith

PREACHED AT BLETCHINGDON
HARVEST FESTIVAL 1962

It isn't true that Public Authorities never get any sense into their heads, because sometimes they do. For instance, they've begun to see that they oughtn't to cut up good agricultural land for housing estates. Why, they even take trouble to put atomic stations on sandy heath, where nothing but birch trees would grow anyway. It's a terrible thing to see good productive land spoilt, even if it's only a bit of garden. At this very time they're building a new Oxford College on a garden I used to have. Well, I suppose I ought to care more about young men getting educated than I do about strawberries and asparagus, but it seems I don't. I just can't bear to see my garden, as it was, turned into a building-site. And it's all the more surprising I should still be so fond of that garden, since my memories of it are war-time memories. We hadn't got much to eat in the year 1940 but what we grew ourselves, and yet how good it was, living off the land, eating or giving away every bit that was fit for food, collecting even the crab-apples from the hedge for jelly. It wasn't only that the stuff was fresh, and tasted good: it was the whole business of living by one's own efforts and working along with nature at first hand.

It is often said that the cultivator's life inclines to religion, because it leaves men in the hands of a power they cannot themselves control. There is no certainty about the seasons and just when you've got the caterpillars taped, in come the pigeons or the squirrels. So you just have to leave it to God. But I do not think that the practical lesson of cultivation is like this at all. The lesson is care and patience. Of course nature springs surprises on you, but it isn't nature's surprises that make the difference between failure and success in the long run. Blight and mildew are controlled by spraying; not begged off by praying, as every farmer knows.

All the same, there is more religion in the country than in the town, for the cultivator experiences nature at first hand. I don't see why we should expect men to be less religious, because they find the God of nature to be faithful, or dependable. It is a barbarous religion, surely, which worships a capricious tyrant. It is the God of the heathen, not the Father of Christ, who sends good and evil at his whim, and is open to be persuaded by prayers or sacrifices. No, God is faithful, is dependable, and the more we find out about nature, the more deeply we explore the faithfulness of God. What seemed caprices to our ignorance become regularities in our better knowledge. The most freakish of thunderstorms has its causes, through which it can be foreseen, and what is foreseen can be forestalled.

Farmers are not the only men whom first-hand acquaintance with nature inclines towards reverence. My own experience, for what it is worth, contradicts a common opinion—the opinion that scientists are atheists. Not at all—there are many believing scientists, especially among the patient researchers into nature's ways. The clever theorist, who constructs an overall picture of the universe, is in danger of an intellectual power-complex—he thinks that his thought is master of the world. But the honest researcher, chipping away patiently at the rock of natural fact, is often moved to reverence by what he handles. For he finds in nature two qualities which human skill scarcely knows how to reconcile or combine—infinite spontaneity and infinite dependableness. Is it surprising that these two qualities, taken together, seem worthy of a divine hand? For what is God, if he is not a faithful creator—infinitely creative, though faithful, or dependable; infinitely faithful, however creative or surprising. We are great fools surely, if we lose the sense of God, simply because we find we can rely on him.

My sisters and I were born in Hampstead, and were brought up by a mother who was so dependable, she was almost like a piece of God's nature herself. The house always went smoothly. There was very little money behind it, but somehow no one was allowed to feel the strain. There were always good meals on time—my mother got very tired, I believe, but she did it somehow. She soothed everyone's troubles and never mentioned her own. If she had made more fuss, I suppose I should have taken more notice: if I had had to do without her, I should have seen what I owed to her. Her goodness made me thoughtless. I remember once thinking it would be fun to drive home from Oxford with three fellow students, who were going far and so wanted to start very early. 'We'll stop at our place,' I said, 'and have breakfast.' I rang my mother up at some terrible hour in the morning and we all landed hungry on the mat. The breakfast was there and my mother smiled. It was only years afterwards that she recalled the occasion, and laughed at me for having been so absurd. She had had practically nothing in the larder.

And so it is the faithfulness of God, his unseen dependableness, which makes us ungrateful. 'Ah, my dear Mother,' I can now say, 'how I wish . . .'—but it is too late.

Anyhow, at a harvest festival we remember our manners for once, and come to thank God for his faithful kindness all the year. Not only we thank him ourselves, we thank him aloud and publicly, and let our neighbours see that we want to do honour to God.

My mother was a good woman—no one more truly a Christian— and I dare say she did not specially want to be made a fuss of, or to hear endless speeches of thanks. She wanted her children to grow and thrive on her kindness, to work along with her efforts in bringing us up. There is a sort of unthankfulness which is far more cruel than an unthankful tongue—and that is, a contempt for people's services to us. Is a cook more hurt by our lack of praise, or by our leaving her food uneaten? The worst ungratefulness to parents is, not asking for their help, not taking their advice; if they give us presents of clothes, not wearing them; if they give us presents of books, not reading them.

So it is with God. The real unthankfulness is pushing away the things he wants to give us most. We accept the material benefits—the sunshine, the rain, the food, and all the powers of nature which he has taught us to use so skilfully. And certainly God wants to give us these things, and loves to see us enjoy them, just as our mother liked to see us eat. For all our happiness is dear to God, and especially if we share it with others and invite them to our table.

But there are things he wants even more to give us—so much so, that he sent his Son to die for us. He wants to give us— how can I say it?—he wants to give us himself. Sunshine and rain, food, drink and medicine will not keep us alive for more than some seventy or eighty years. If God shares his life with us, it will keep us alive for ever. But only if the life of God gets under our skins, and makes us divine. We have to grow together into one with Christ, for God is in Christ already.

So it is no true gratitude to God if we thank him for rain, sunshine, air, medicine and food, while we push away the things he died to give us—the holy sacrament week by week, the good gifts and helps with daily living which God longs to put into our hearts, if only we will open them to him by praying steadily. Look, he says to us, you have found how to rely on my faithfulness in the things of the body: come and try me in the life of the soul. I am faithful, and I have promised to bless. You think your heart is hard, that you can't repent and start religion over again, but come and see. Pour out your heart to me, make your confession, and see if I will not forgive you and set you back on the good path.

Religion is all concerned with the faithfulness of God and with the unfaithfulness of men. We lose heart in religion, because we think we can trust ourselves to be faithful to God. We break down and then we are discouraged. No, religion is not pretending to be faithful, it is trust in the faithfulness of God, and going back to him again and again and again for forgiveness and a fresh start.

So, then, we have come here to thank God for his goodness. But there is only one sort of thanks he cares for, and that is, that we should use his most precious gifts, and not despise what he died to give us. 'I've been dying to get to know you', people sometimes say to a new acquaintance, and heaven knows what they mean. But Christ died to get to know us, or (since he knows us already) he died to bring us into fellowship with him. 'Behold', he says, 'I stand at the door and knock. If any man will open, I will come in, and share his supper; and he shall share mine.'

Also preached at St Mary's, Primrose Hill, London, 1963.

Supporting Hands

> Jacob was left alone;
> and there wrestled a man with him
> until the breaking of the day.
> And he that wrestled with him said:
> Let me go, for the day breaketh,
> And Jacob said, I will not let thee go,
> except thou bless me. GEN. 32.24–26

Have you noticed how in railway stations and some other such places vintage advertisements mysteriously linger, and by their antique phrasing, raise a smile? My eye fell on such a caption—perhaps you have seen it: FOR LADIES, FOR UPLIFT AND GENERAL SUPPORT. I was thunderstruck. Good heavens, I said to myself, what can these people be trying to sell? Surely it must be the established religion.

These are the things that it is commonly thought to be for. 'For ladies, for uplift, and for general support.' *For ladies*—we all know that the practice of piety is ladylike, and is especially appropriate if the lady is not young. *For uplift*—well, there are after all occasions when others beside ladies of advancing years need to have their confidence in their own virtue bolstered up, and their hearts made to glow; and a bit of religious oratory and community hymn-singing is the very thing for the purpose. And then—*for general support*. There is something called the western way of life, which we all are supposed to approve, but it seems to be sagging rather at the knees. What it wants is general support, and a measure of belief in Christian values will give it just the support it needs.

And so, do you see, the advertisement I saw was an excellent advertisement, for an advertisement should be addressed to the mind of the time and so it seemed to be. Only seemed, for as a matter of fact my thoughts were running on too fast.

I looked at the advertisement more carefully, and saw that it was not issued by the Wayside Pulpit, or any other of the presses who publicize piety. The object was to sell some sort of thing that ties round the waist. But never mind. I had seen what I had seen, and I began thinking about keeping in step with the times, and advertising religion. After all, it's my job, isn't it? Suppose they say to me, write us an advertisement to stick up in the bus. What shall I say? I take up my pen and try to write it, but my pen will not move. I try to shape a set of words in my mouth, and nothing comes. How do we advertise our faith? What is it good for?

Good for everything, I dare say, but it is irrelevant, blasphemous, to recommend it so. There is none good, said Christ, but one only, God; and I greatly doubt whether my faith is any good to him, he needs nothing. This one thing I know, that it is good for me to cleave to God, which is only another way of saying, to have faith in him.

Advertisements for faith, however much they may conceal the fact, treat the Creator of the Universe as a useful tool for achieving human ends. We, as men, find it a nuisance, perhaps, that we cannot leave our suitcases on the rack without having them opened. The level of public honesty must be dangerously low. Never mind, there is a medicine for it which is confidently recommended by the higher clergy—interdenominational Christianity administered in an educational spoon. Being partially predigested it is readily assimilated.

But God is not for us, that is, he is not a medicine in our cupboard nor a weapon in an armoury. We are for him. It is our calling, says a Christian writer, to be to the Divine Majesty what a man's right hand is to a man. But the Bible speaks of us more humbly, not as hands, but as instruments: 'Shall the axe lift itself', says the Prophet, 'against him that wields it?' That is, the creature against his God. We can have no religion, while we think that religion may be good for us, instrumental to us. Suppose we write an up-to-date version of the Prodigal Son. He knocks at the door, and the father looks out. 'Why, Fred', he says. 'Yes, it's me', says the son. 'I've just arrived by the afternoon plane. You see I did all right at first, over there in Terra Longinqua, but then I began to develop some awkward habits: kleptomania, I couldn't keep my hands off other people's things; getting drunk; extravagance; sexual oddities; and then I had dreams. The long and the short of it was, I consulted a psychiatrist. It's father-trouble, he says. You've got a guilt complex about the old man. You must go home, and re-establish some sort of relation; it's your only medicine!' 'Oh, I'm your medicine, am I?' says the father. That is not how Christ's parable goes. True, the son is moved to return by the sense of his poverty, his dissatisfaction, nothing to put in his belly but chaff. But as he approaches his ancient home, all that goes out of his mind. He has before his eyes only the father he must meet. And this sounds better, does it not, than our imaginary version: 'Father, I have sinned against heaven and in thy sight, and am no more worthy to be called thy son.' And this of the Father's is better, too: 'Bring forth the best robe, and put it on him, a ring for his hand, shoes for his feet. Slay the fatted calf, let us feast and be merry. For this my son was dead and is alive again, was lost and is found.'

Religion is the service of God, faith is cleaving to God. God cannot be served, cannot be cleaved to, except for his own sake and because he is God. There is no advertisement for faith, no commendation of faith, but this testimony: we know that we have run away from God in vain, have forgotten him in vain, have delayed our repentances in vain. But we have been pulled back, made to remember, forced to repent, by our natural master, in whose service our true being lies.

All of us who have been brought up within the faith of Christ have had some time before our eyes an absolute holiness, which commands the obedience of our will. This is not a fiction, not a fairy tale about some power up in heaven, but a reality that presses on us here. It is in fact, omnipotence; but Almighty God is pleased to wrestle with us gently, as he did with Jacob in the old Hebrew tale. And when we are young (and often afterwards) we twist and turn, and try to put him off. We tell ourselves that what grasps us is only a dream of our own, or our inherited code of duty. And indeed we do dream many things falsely of God, and see his will distorted by various conventions. But, he says to us, 'a thousand veils may hide me, and yet I am here. Everything you think of me is false, but you know that, whatever I am, you have me to wrestle with. You can run away if you like, and go on hiding from me till you're old. But if you know and face me, you must wrestle with me; and if you wrestle with me, I shall break your dreams about me first, and then (for I am Almighty) I shall break your heart.

'You will be heart-broken before the face of my holiness, because I am your Father, and you are not, and cannot be, worthy to be called my son. But I have said it, a broken and a contrite heart I will not despise; and the breaking of the heart is the opening of Heaven.' Jesus, coming up out of the water of his baptism, saw the sky broken over his head, and through that rent the voice came down to him of a measureless acceptance, 'Thou art my beloved Son, in thee I am content.' He by desert, but we by mercy, through the breaking of our world, the breaking of our heart, receive the adoption of sons.

The evidence of faith (I talk of what I think I know) is the evidence of Almighty Power, to break and heal the will. And if we want to put it to the test, this is required of us: not to run away from God, but to face him and hold back the curtains of insincerity with steady hands, begging him for the truth about himself and us. And we shall come to know that whatever is a dream, this which takes hold of us is not a dream. Those who believe are those who cannot but believe.

Our salvation cannot be achieved without the use of force; and when I say salvation, I mean that of which damnation is the alternative. It is salvation to be laid hold of by God, and there is no guarantee that if we throw away our present opportunities, they can be endlessly renewed for us. Our salvation cannot be achieved without the use of force. Essentially the force is God's, but to expose ourselves to his force we must put force upon ourselves. You can find the example in the life of any saint. St Vincent de Paul has been popularized as the founder of organized charity before the welfare state. What has not been so widely popularized is that the man rose summer and winter every day at four o'clock, and held his mind for three hours facing God in his prayer: after which he started his fourteen hours a day of work for the criminal, the ignorant, and the destitute. Such achievements are not for us. Still, the example may make us think. If we are too lazy to pray for a matter of minutes before we go to breakfast, too careless or too mean to buy an alarm clock that we may be sure to rise and receive the sacrament well-prepared one day in seven, we are scarcely treating our religion with the seriousness of grown men, not to say our God with the honour due to a creator. Nor are we exposing our wills sufficiently to the grasp which must master them. I will not let thee go, says Jacob, except thou bless me: and how willing that mysterious wrestler is to bless. It is not on him we practise mastery, but on ourselves, when we say, I will not let thee go.

One leaf is written on the reverse side of a letter from the Reverend J. C. Stephenson, dated 30 September 1949.

Inspiration by the Spirit

I had five aunts who lived together in a Hampstead house known to their nephews and nieces as the Aunt-Heap. They were extremely charitable, and never was there a household of people who so consistently bought cabbages from bad greengrocers because their wives suffered from varicose veins, or employed slatternly charwomen because their husbands were supposed to be reclaimed drunkards. Their numerous fringe of casual employees were known by us collectively as the Old Frauds. One object of their charity was an indigent cousin of some kind who was bed-ridden. If you visited her you would sooner or later—and a good deal sooner than later—hear her tale of woe. A doctor had recommended the amputation of her leg at the knee and promised to set her upright on a wooden peg. 'But', said cousin Harriet, 'that very night the Holy Ghost said to me, "Miss Barker, don't you have it off." ' With the result that she was useless to herself, and a care to others, for the remaining forty years of her life. No doubt an edifying conclusion.

We will now get on the time machine and come some forty years nearer to the present day. A young woman joined an enthusiastic religious group which ran like wildfire round the world in the twenties and thirties. In the solvent atmosphere of a shared emotion she fell in love with a man formerly of bad life whom the group had converted. But just as the wedding began to look like practical politics she was seized with terrible misgivings. Did the man genuinely love her and would it last? She made the mistake of sharing her anxiety with the group, with which, indeed, she was taught to share all things. Theirs was a meeting of communal quiet. They laid it before the Lord and they waited for guidance. The leader uttered the oracle; and it was the current saying in the group, that the leader's guidance was always right. The Spirit declared that the marriage was to go forward. The girl's fears were groundless. It was a marriage in the Lord, it would consecrate their union with the fellowship and keep them steadfast in the Lord's work. Very edifying; but the husband quickly relapsed into his evil life, cursed the Christian group with all his heart, brought his mistresses into his house, and drove out his two children and his wife. The woman, being brave and steadfast, worked and brought up her children. So the human race got two recruits out of the mess, for it is God's way to bring his good out of our evil. I find it hard to believe, however, that the evil was the intention of his holy will in the first place.

The two cases I've narrated to you are both true fact, and the comparison between them is instructive. Old cousin Harriet followed her heart: the young woman went against hers. What hit cousin Harriet with the force of divine authority was something which came rushing up from the bottom of her mind, and I could put a name to it—so could you—it was animal fear, the fear of the surgeon's knife. What overbore the unlucky young bride was group support for the leader's ideas; and his ideas did not come so much from the heart, as from the head. The reason why the group held that Dick's guidance was always right was that he had an uncanny skill in planning an evangelistic campaign, so as to obtain visible success in the short run. And so, I suppose, he was doing in the case of this unfortunate engagement of marriage. He was, as was habitual with him, seeing it as part of his group tactics. Marriages within the group tended to hold the group together; and especially to tie in a man of popular gifts, a potentially useful agent of propaganda who was, however, dangerously unstable. So he sacrificed the individual to the collective plan, like any communist.

So, in the one case the heart seized control, in the other the head. What, then, was the matter? We know very well that we've got to listen to our heart, and also to our head; there's no folly in attending to either. The common error in the two cases was simply a mistaken belief in inspiration. You could not argue with cousin Harriet's fear, and what was worse, she couldn't argue with it herself. For she must not resist the Holy Ghost, lest she be found to be fighting against God. And so with Dick's guidance: once it was acclaimed as the voice of God, it was irresistible. The young lady should have been free to say: I see the force of Dick's view—it is perfectly true that marriages within the group are helpful to the group and to its evangelistic work, but only if these marriages are sound. Now as to whether this marriage in particular is sound, neither Dick nor any other member of the group is so well placed for judging as I am. It is I who feel the quality of the man's attitude to me and it fills me with a misgiving which no amount of argument can quiet or dispel.

The trouble about an indiscreet belief in inspiration is that it smothers reason. A man who declares 'This is what the Spirit directs' is not required to give a reason; surely God does not argue his cases. But I say to you, always suspect claims to inspired guidance which bypass reasoned argument. There are not fewer reasons for what God ordains than for other things; there are more, far more. There are all the reasons in the world, if we can but find them. For is not he wise?

If I were sitting where you sit, and hearing the preacher produce these old skeletons out of the family cupboard, I think that I should be saying something like this. 'The man is talking common sense and flat worldly wisdom, and I wouldn't want to dispute it on that level. Only what he is saying amounts to this—that the Christian Gospel isn't true, but quite false. For the Gospel promises us the Holy Spirit to guide us; whereas the preacher says that no belief can be more dangerous than the belief that we have the guidance of the Spirit.' If, in fact, any of you are sharing any such protest as that, I agree that it's a perfectly fair challenge and as such I propose to take it up.

Is the Christian inspired? Yes, he is indeed. Just as inspired as he is Christian, and just as Christian as he is inspired. Are we not told that the Spirit is Christ's other self and that the Spirit in us is the very overflow of Christ's divine life? And, as St Paul says, putting it negatively, those that are not led by the Spirit of Christ are none of his, that is, they are not Christians at all. Only *how* does the Spirit of Christ shape our spirits? I am going, in answer, to give you a very dull word, a word which has no poetic colour or emotional aura—the word is, *attitude*. The Christian who seeks in prayer and sacrament the company of Christ, who puts himself into the acts and concerns of Christ, is drawn quite without consciousness, perhaps, into the attitudes of Christ. And Christ's attitude is a two-sided relationship: to his divine Father, and to his human brothers. The so-called Christian virtues are attitudes— Christ's attitudes passing over into us, to become ours. Attitudes, for example, of faith, of hope, of love. These attitudes, so far as we Christians share them, are simply Christlike, simply divine, and no inspiration we could possibly receive could be higher or diviner than this. There is nothing better, in this life, that God could give us.

The attitudes are the basic things, the immediate form of the divine life in us. But then, of course, they carry with them many particular illuminations. The mind governed by Christ's faith, Christ's hope, Christ's love, is the mind that sees straight, and so the convert cries with the blind man healed in the Gospel story: 'I was blind; and now I see!' Of course conversion to Christ brings spiritual perceptiveness: for it teaches us to look through the eyes of God!

Between getting one's spiritual eyes, and claiming oracular inspirations, the difference is wide. Oracular assurances are a *substitute* for intellectual sight, whereas what we are talking about is a clearing of intellectual sight. A good pair of spectacles is not a substitute for the use of one's eyes. When I have the advantage of spectacles, I do not say, 'My spectacles tell me so-and-so', but, 'I see such-and-such a state of affairs'. My spectacles do not inform me, they make my sense perfect, so that the visible world may inform me. The Christian mind quickened by faith, hope and love is simply capable of a greater perceptiveness. Heaven help the Christian whose prayers do not make him quicker of eye to appreciate another's need, and to hear the call of duty as it arises in every circumstance of life! The Christian whose prayers make him more shut up in himself, less open to the glory of the world or to the image of God in his fellows, what sort of a Christian is he? And to what can he be praying? Surely to wood or stone, and not to the living God, the Father of our Lord Jesus Christ.

We say in the Creed, I believe in the Holy Ghost, the lifegiver, who spoke through the prophets. The two functions are one. How did he speak through the prophets? How else than by making them all alive? And when they were alive, then they were alive to what surrounded them, and alive to what God was doing and declaring in their days, and so what they saw they could not but speak.

Well, this is very fine, and if God did no more for us than make us divinely alive to himself and to one another, we might think he had done all we would dare to ask. But does not he do

more? Does he not (for all I may say) give his servants special
inspiration, showing them things about their call or their destiny
which they could never gather from looking round on the world,
never mind with how clear or enlightened eyes? Well, yes, he does.
I will fish another rag out of my family dustbin for you—a very
commonplace example. There was my little old aunt Ellen. She
did not join the Aunt-Heap until long after cousin Harriet's time—
not until she was old. Till then she had somewhere else to be,
and something else to do. She was the tiniest creature—as small
as a mouse, and as timid. In her girlhood she fainted at every sight
of blood. But steadily through her teens the conviction grew in
her that Christ would have her to go to India as a missionary
doctor. Not that there were any missionary doctors of her sex
then; the medical schools only opened to women in the year she
was ready to enter. So she went—and I will not enlarge on the
story of her life. I will merely say that if we can be voted into
Paradise by the voices of the poor, my little aunt will have had an
easy passage. But all that's irrelevant. I have only to speak now of
her resolution, or conviction about her calling, slowly maturing
in patience and fidelity, with no excitement, no tension, no oracles
from the skies, but a growing sense of what God meant to make of
her, and through her. And so, perhaps, God will give you assurance
of the calling he has for you; and this, I say, is a manner of inspiration which goes somewhat beyond the mere sharpening of our
eyes to see what is around us.

Just now I gave you a word: attitude. And now I will give
you another—depth. The sharing of the Lord's attitude of heart
and mind through prayer is not just Yes or No—you either share
it or you don't—it's a matter of depth. We can enter deeply, or
shallowly, into the divine-human life of Christ. Rather like pro-
posing a retreat. Well, a retreat with its silence, its concentration
on God, its mutual support of the participants in seeking him—
what is it, but an opportunity to reach a depth which, perhaps,
you never conceived of? Of course, those of you who have never
been on retreat may be terrified at the idea. But terrified of what?
Of God? Or of emptiness, and of finding no God there? He will
be there, have no fear: and in complete quietness, without stress
or excitement, he will open to you a new depth in the wells of
life.

A Father's Begetting

Only three more days to go, for our poor pupils in the Schools—and what a relief when it's over! How some of them do work themselves up, to be sure! I wonder how they can be so silly, which only shows what a short memory I have. For who am I, to pity the present generation of schoolsmen with such an Olympian detachment? The last time I competed in Schools, what happened? By sitting late over Greek print in a badly lighted library, I finished my eyes and Schools together. I was forbidden to read for three months. Not read for three months? What was I to do? 'Look,' said my father, 'the fence round the garden is falling to pieces, we'll replace it. We'll do it in oak; and we won't buy the uprights ready slotted, we'll cut them out with hand tools.' So we made that solid oak paling right round the garden, my father and I. I wonder whether it still stands? The weeks flew by, the long sunshiny days of satisfying manual labour. I never had a happier summer than that summer I was supposed to be blind. There was the pleasure of doing a great work, and overcoming hourly difficulties. But above all, there was the pleasure of working with my father, who did not make himself the boss—he accepted me as an equal. All the time there was the feeling of his kindness, who had undertaken such a labour to keep me cheerful; but there was nothing indebting in it, it was so obvious he enjoyed the work as much as I did. My zest, however great, could not equal his. And anyhow, in the case of my father, I had never even begun to dream of worrying about his doing me favours. His idea of being happy was getting mixed up in his children's affairs. Why, a few years before that, when he saw me getting miserable over Latin verses, he actually mastered the technique of Ovidian elegiacs, which they had never taught him at school, so that he could help me twist my bad Latin prose into worse pentameters.

I know that it is all very well for me to go on like this, but that there may be no answering recollection in my audience—some of you don't have much to do with your fathers, and some of you wish you had less to do with them than you have. They were angels to you when you were small, but you've grown up into very different sort of animals. You know it's only decent to make them think that you are devoted to them, but it's hard work. You can't be their children any longer, and you can't be their friends yet. All the same, you are sorry, and you see what a pleasure it would be, if that dear body which begot you could house the heart of your most familiar friend.

I met a man the other day and he gave me a preposterous great lunch in a hotel. I said to him, 'How do you manage to be so disgustingly rich?' He replied, 'Well, to start with, I was very careful in the choice of a father', and then went on into the mysteries of the real-estate market. His opening remark was no doubt meant for a joke, our paternity being about the one thing in which we have no choice. And yet, of course, in a secondary sense you do choose fathers. Sometimes you find such a figure in a friend not very much older than yourself, but more experienced. The young men who write for the *Isis* and the *Cherwell* would maintain that it never is your dons that you put to such a use, though sometimes you are so nice as to flatter us into the belief that it is so; and that is highly gratifying. But some of you— and those are the lucky ones—make a father *of your father*, and only he knows how gratifying that is to him, for God and nature have predisposed his heart in your favour. And I do hope that those of you who are having a sticky passage with your fathers, and have not got over the very necessary but painful business of achieving independence from paternal tyranny, will do all you can to re-establish relations on a basis of equality as soon as possible. Do it, while the going is good: you will not have your fathers always. When my present College was so kind as to suggest my coming into it, how I should have liked to talk to my father about it, but alas!

Do you ever write to your fathers? It is an amiable and can even be an enjoyable exercise. There is a special reason. God has made known to us the mysteries of his kindness through human parables. But what makes these parables so forcible, is that they are not merely parables we can grasp, but parables we must enact. That is why they get right in amongst us. He has given us the friendship of Father and Son, on a level of equality—*nihil in hac Trinitate vel maius vel minus*—as the clue to the most august of mysteries, the life of the Godhead. It is hard for us to worship the divine reality, if we are falsifying in our own person the human parable: if we are ungrateful or indifferent sons to our earthly fathers. I am so sorry for those of you who have to try to be otherwise; I never had to try at all. My little blind soul, nosing its way into the world, had been so careful in the choice of a father.

Of course the living parable can be translated into terms of *other* relationships—some of you can make nothing much of your fathers, however hard you try, and some of you have no fathers surviving. You are not condemned by that to a practical ignorance of God. The one lived-out parable which is inescapable is that which St John has stated for us: 'If a man says "I love God" and hates his brother man, he lies. For he who loves not the man he sees, the God he cannot see how is he to love?' The general parable will do, only the parable has a special force—to love a heavenly Father in loving an earthly; and if we have an earthly father whom we will not love, then St John's words will come home to us in the special application. If a man loves not the father he sees with his eyes, how should he love the Father invisible? He is a liar if he pretends it.

For the same principle is involved in both cases: that we should acknowledge the pit from which we were digged and love the author of our being. Only that the authorship of our being does not mean the same thing in the two relationships. My father was the physical cause of my presence in this world; even if he had died before I was born, I should still have been here. As it happened, he contributed greatly to that second begetting, the waking of mind in me. He talked me into talking, and by thinking aloud to me, taught me to think. And again, to a third begetting, the last of the three: he put me in the way of knowing God, and then stood out of the light of that ray which comes from heaven, and which no man, even the dearest of fathers, can communicate.

But although a father may do all this to us, and though his memory may remain a frequent inspiration, yet the effect of his creative activity is to set us on our own feet. We had our being from him; we do not continue to draw it from such a source. We replace our fathers; they die in the course of nature, we have children of our own, if we are so blest. But the heavenly Father of the heavenly Son remains the perpetual source, out of which he draws his being like water from a fountain. There is no other well of life, no origin of existence but this. The Son is equal to the Father—there is nothing in the spring which does not come out in the stream; and yet wholly derived from him—there is nothing in the stream, but what that spring pours into it.

And so there enters into the heavenly pattern of fatherhood and sonship an element absent from the earthly pattern: the substance and life of Godhead constantly poured from the Father into the Son—the Holy Ghost. The earthly pattern of father and son is a duality, the heavenly pattern is a blessed and indivisible Trinity. This is so, because the Father of the heavenly Son is not only his father, but his God.

We were agreeing just now that, in a manner of speaking, we choose our fathers on earth, and that it is a happy thing if we find a father in our father. How astonishing that the same liberty belongs to us in relation to the Father of our souls! Only that here, the adoption of substitutes is never tolerable. If we adhere to any other, it is a sterile idolatry. We have deserted the fountain of living waters, like the poor Jews whom Christ rebuked, who said that God was their father, but had made themselves faithful children to the prince of pride and lies, as very soon appeared, when they crucified the true Son whom the heavenly Father had sent them.

Even the divine Son himself, under the conditions of our mortal life, was faced with this momentous choice, and was tempted as we are. His whole action on earth was a steady adopting of his Father *as* his father, a perseverance in loyalty and dependence, a standing firm in the direct stream of the Holy Ghost, even when failure was the reward, torture the price, and death the end.

The pains were great, but the joy was immeasurable. What was his pleasure in working with his heavenly Father, as he had once worked with Joseph in their common carpentry? I suppose they must have built fences together, too. But now it was another fence, not made with hands, in which the Father and the Son laboured as one; a fence to fence out Satan from Paradise, and hedge a road for us to the tree of life.

The heart of being, the blessed Trinity above all worlds, is not a mystery by which the knowledge of Godhead is withheld from our enquiring minds. It is a pattern of life into which we ourselves, by an unspeakable mercy, are taken up. For Christ joins us with himself in the continual, practical, daily choice of his Father as our father. Why, he makes us part of himself, he calls us his members, his eyes and tongue, his hands and feet. He puts us where he is, in Sonship to his Father, and opens to us the inexhaustible and all-quickening fountain, the spirit of Sonship, the river of life, the Holy Ghost.

Preached on Trinity Sunday 1961; also at St Edmund Hall, Oxford, Michaelmas Term, 1963.

Signs and Wonders

One of those pathetic illusions from which clergymen suffer is the belief that people take notice of what is said from the pulpit. So the conscientious preacher corrects his own mistakes. 'I told you last Sunday that Elisha was fed by ravens. I should, of course, have said Elijah.' 'Eh, what's that?' says the churchwarden to his wife. 'Can't remember anything about it. Anyhow, Molly, don't you try feeding me no ravens. They aren't wholesome.'

Well, it's all too true that people go to sleep in sermons, but even if they keep awake there's no particular need for them to memorize what they hear. It is the vanity of preachers to suppose that their audiences come to listen to them; they don't, of course; they come to listen to God. That is certainly a rather solemn way of putting it. The churchwarden whom I have just quoted is not likely to say anything like that. But he knows what it is to 'enjoy' a sermon. You suspect him of emotional frivolity—he enjoys it if his feelings are tickled. Nothing of the kind; he is a more serious man than you are. He enjoys it, if in the course of his hearing it some divine reality comes alive to him, and God makes a touch upon his soul. The effect may be sternly practical: he repents a sin, or remembers a duty, or thinks more kindly of a neighbour. This is the work of God. It may have no direct or logical relation to what the preacher said, yet the preacher did not speak in vain.

But another well-known truth about preachers is that they don't themselves practise what they preach. So you won't be surprised to hear me act contrary to what I've just said, and talk as though you *would* remember a remark I made this morning. There is, indeed, special warrant tonight for serving up the cold remains of this morning's feast, for the New Testament lesson this evening picks up this morning's gospel, and caps the first miracle of Cana in Galilee with the story of the second. Well now, in comment on the first miracle I said that we could not hope to know at this remove of time just what the miracle was, and anyhow 'miracle' wasn't the point. And ever since, I wonder whether you haven't been thinking it was a cheat. What about the miracle? If that is your line, you have powerful backing. Our wise Archbishops concur in setting us a lesson this evening which gives us two more miracles. If *you* do not want to let me off, neither, it seems, do the two Archbishops, founded as they are in the support of the Convocations both of Canterbury and of York.

What, then, about gospel miracles? The modern Catholic Church has a scientific procedure for sifting true miracles from false. Myriads of invalids go on the pilgrimage to Lourdes and very few of them are healed. Never mind, those who aren't healed in the body receive spiritual benefits and even a few healings are enough to show the hand of God, if, that is, they *are* miracles. But are they? The Church knows perfectly well the possibility of psychological cure. Many people are ill because they haven't the courage to be well. It is a very proper function of the Lourdes pilgrimage that it should give them the courage, and make them well. Excellent, but that's not miracle. So a panel of doctors and physiologists, some of them Christians and some of them not, is called in to examine alleged cases of miraculous cure. And these learned men do sift out a small number of cases about which they say, that no known principles of science will explain them. They may even go further, and say that it would greatly surprise them if scientific principles ever were discovered that would explain them. And so these cases are solemnly recorded as miracles.

I must say that the business of the Lourdes miracles is of fascinating interest and no doubt the evidence, if genuine, proves something or other of importance, though it's so difficult to see what. Anyhow, whatever it is, the Lourdes phenomenon isn't a bit of the New Testament turning up in this modern world; Lourdes is a purely modern development. The miraculousness of gospel miracles was not tested against the explanatory powers of science, for there was no such science. Not only hadn't they got the science, they hadn't even got the idea.

Suppose now we take a look at the two miracles in tonight's lesson. The first story is the story of a healing from a distance: Jesus did not even visit the house of sickness. And so, you might say, the cure is doubly miraculous. But look, the child is in the crisis of a dangerous fever. Either he'll die, or he'll fall into a healthful sleep and his temperature will go down. It is the latter that happens. Jesus wanted the anxious parent simply to trust in God. Being pressed, he gave way, feeling sorry for the man, and assures him his child was mending at that moment. The man went home, and found that it was so. What shall we say that Jesus did? Did he have insight into the will of God for the child, a will with which he was marvellously at one? Did he pray for the child? Did he use a gift of second sight which is, after all, not so uncommon as rationalists think?

It is with a fever-crisis as it was with the squall on the Galilean Lake. Squalls on lakes cease as suddenly as they come on. Jesus wanted his disciples not to worry. They pressed him, he spoke the word of power. Did he think that he was co-operating with God's will in nature, or opposing it?

Our other story, that of the man crippled with paralysis, is different. A long-established paralysis does not just go, like a fever. Christ healed no paralytic from a distance. The intervention of the healer was required. But certain crippled conditions yield to psychological force. There were invalids who astonished their nurses by running downstairs in air raids. St John, who tells us the story, appears to assume that the man might have been healed anyhow if he could only have got into the magic spring at the magic moment. The trouble is, he can't. But a word from Christ is as good, or better. The moral seems to be, that in the old religion people had to wait for set times and seasons to get the healing of God. Now it is always available, for we can always turn to Christ.

After saying the sort of things that I have just said about the Gospel miracles, it is usual with theologians to add, 'Ah, but the really important thing about the stories is the light they cast on the disciples' view of Christ.' I don't agree. The point is of very secondary interest. The supremely important thing is the attitude of Christ himself. Surely he saw himself as a worker of miracles. What did he think he was doing?

We must boldly say of Jesus that he inherited and used a stock of old-world ideas, many of which we have discarded. It was not this period-stuff that made his thinking divine. The divine thing was what he did with it.

So then, Jesus inherited a picture of nature and of history in which God just does everything that is done. For the most part, he does it invisibly, and that is when we would say that natural law is taking its course. But sometimes God shows his hand and calls a human instrument, say a prophet, to enter into his intentions and to forward them. When this happened, no one bothered to ask whether natural causes were present or absent, or whether they would have sufficed of themselves to produce the effect. The supreme miracle of the Old Testament was Israel's escape from Egypt. What had happened? A stray hot wind, blowing all night, pushed the shallow water off the sands of Suez. The Israelites slipped across under cover of dark. The Egyptian chariotry followed at the crack of dawn, their wheels stuck in the sand and the water came back on them. Only Moses was inspired to will with the will of God and to lead Israel over.

The question of scientific explanations didn't arise because it was a practical, not a speculative, matter. It was a matter of discerning what in fact the divine will was set to do, and of making yourself its instrument. What God was doing had, no doubt, all sorts of scientific bearings; the inspired man did not need to know them. If Jesus could feel the force of vitality in the cripple and his capacity for faith, and the will of God moving to his deliverance, he could put himself into the hand of God and make the man well. To take an analogy: there are all sorts of scientific questions about the production of my voice and about the psychology of my attitude to my sermon, but you can cut all that out if you care to appreciate what I mean to say.

So the activity of Jesus is the direct appreciation of God's saving action, and the coming in on it. Or rather, he didn't have to come in on it, for he lived in it; that's where he was. Oh well, he slept sometimes, and he rested; and then he had to come back into it, yes. The saving action of God sometimes impelled him to play a part in which nothing more happened than a prediction that a fever-patient would recover. Sometimes it impelled him to speak words of power arousing the faith that heals. Sometimes, I believe, the tide of the divine grace carried him beyond all boundaries known to us, and did wonderful things we cannot explain.

I will give you a formula: Jesus experimented with Omnipotence, and let it find its own limits. Maybe there were things that Divine Love would not do, because God loves the order of the world, as well as the happiness of men. But Jesus had nothing to fear. He would be shown as he went, he would know within himself, what it pleased Almighty Love to do.

This is the same Jesus who went through disaster and death into immortal resurrection. This is the invincible Christ who says, 'Be of good cheer: I have conquered the world.'

The gospel and lesson referred to are for Epiphany 2.

Conscience

PREACHED IN PUSEY HOUSE OXFORD 1966

So I'm to talk about Conscience. Conscience! What on earth are we to say about Conscience? We can't do with it, and yet we can't do without it. We can't do with it, it's the awkwardest thing. If a man will hear reason, we can hope to make some sense of him. If he takes his stand on conscience, there's no argument possible. It was the custom of a College to which I belonged to admit new Fellows to their fellowships in the College Chapel. But then here was a conscientious atheist. His conscience wouldn't let him promise to be a good boy, or to receive a handshake from the head of the College—not in that accursed building. 'It's all right,' we said to him, 'no one's going to pray at you, and everyone knows you're no Christian. We shall all realize you are merely being agreeable to the rest of us, doing the usual thing.' 'That sounds fair enough,' he says, 'but my conscience is against it.' Surely no one ever took his stand on conscience, if he had a reason to give, for if he had, he'd give the reason. Let us suppose that the Good Samaritan's ass, like Balaam's, finds a tongue. 'Come on, master,' she says, 'you'll be late for supper and I could do with a mangerful myself. What's a roadside accident to do with us?' Can you imagine the Samaritan replying: 'Sorry, old lady, I can't turn the blind eye: my conscience won't let me.' Of course not. He'd say, 'But can't you see the man's hurt? If we leave him there, he'll die.' People don't talk about conscience when they've got a reason. They talk about conscience when they mean to be awkward.

So, as I began by saying, we can't do with conscience. But then, on the other hand, we can't do without it. A man without conscience is too unreliable. He may think very clearly, and even public-spiritedly, when he happens to think, but suppose he doesn't happen to? 'It didn't occur to me that you'd be wanting your bicycle this morning.' 'Oh, didn't it? But didn't you feel a twinge of conscience about pinching it without leave asked?' 'Sorry, I'm afraid I don't go in much for guilty twinges. You see, I was very sensibly brought up.' So if conscience is the very devil, *no conscience* is the deep blue sea. What shall we do between the two? Shall we attempt a cocktail—three of conscience to two of unconscientiousness, with a bit of lemon-peel thrown in? But that's nonsense, surely. Conscience claims absolute authority, if you are to have it at all; you can't tell conscience not to speak out of turn.

No, it can't be a question of *how much* conscience. It's a question of conscience's proper job. It's not conscience's job to do duty in place of reason; what is it, then?

Conscience isn't thought. It's a feeling of guilt or wrongness, connected with ingrained moral habits. And its first function is a warning. It *may* be the right thing to borrow James's bicycle without asking James, but the twinge of conscience reminds you that acts of this sort require justification. Is there sufficient reason in the present occasion for setting aside the general rule? The one thing certainly not justifiable is to set conscience aside without thinking out the case.

Second, conscience comes in at the end of the thinking, to help us judge. Can we feel right, or innocent, about doing what we propose, when we've done our thinking? If not, we'd better think again. Our reasons have got to convince our conscience if we're thinking to ourselves, and they've got to convince our neighbour's conscience if we are appealing to him. That's why we don't state conscience itself as a reason: why should your neighbour feel it right, because you tell him you feel it right? Tell him your reason, and see if he feels it right too, or not.

Third, conscience protects us against self-deception. How easily could Joseph have convinced himself that it would be a charitable action to relieve Lady Potiphar of her frustrations! But still it felt all wrong, and perhaps it was only after Joseph had lost his shirt and run for his life, that he realized why it wouldn't do. Could he betray his master's trust? Could he help the lady break her vows or wreck her marriage? Not to mention his own integrity, or his loyalty to the God of Israel. Conscience is no substitute for thought. It is often a check on superficial thinking though, and on self-deception. And how necessary, for self-deception is a school in which we could all of us take first-class degrees.

But here am I, gassing away like an old Greats tutor on conscience and reason, and forgetting that I was put up here to talk about conscience's witness to God. Well, there are a few minutes still to go, so I'll ask you to wash out everything I've said, and start again, for I'm sure that everything I've said tends flat in the wrong direction. How can conscience witness to God, if conscience is just ingrained moral habit coming back on us in the form of feeling? You can't say, 'There must be a God, for if there isn't, who planted conscience in the soil of our minds?' For it may be quite sufficient to reply, our parents planted it, our infant school teacher planted it. The *fact* of conscience is not an argument with which to convince unbelievers that they have a God—or, to speak less absurdly, to convince unbelievers of the God who has them. Conscience is merely an inculcated rule, a rule which has got under our skin—and who can tell what mayn't have got under our skin? Ah, but that's just it—what may not have got under our skin? And suppose *God* has got under our skin! They will say to us, 'Your conscience, after all, is just a Christian conscience; it's nothing more nor less than faith under the skin.' So they will tell us, and if we're wise we shan't quarrel with that. Faith under the skin! But that's just when faith really is faith—when it gets under the skin. What is more characteristic of faith, than to get under the skin?

There are only two possible testimonies to God. First, that God should testify to himself, and second, that our being should cry out in response to our maker; that our whole existence at every level should give witness of his unique power to penetrate, to possess, and to activate us. Who is to be impressed by God on the lips; by the carefully guarded answers Christians give when they are questioned about their belief? But God under the skin—the divine principle become instructive to the heart—there is a witness indeed.

Not that Christians, any more than other men, are excused the pain of thought, or the exploration of moral dilemmas. The level of conscience or of divine instinct in a saint shows how far Christ's conquest of his heart has progressed. It does not show how that conquest has been achieved. A saint enters into the mind of Christ as alone a mind can be entered or possessed, and that is by thinking; by thinking especially those effortful thoughts of which the expression lies in deeds, not in words, and of which prayer is the nature and the form. But in proportion as Christ's mind possesses his, the conscience guiding a man's immediate acts becomes Christian: the lineaments of his master are expressed in the grace of his conduct, and in the very show of his face. Do we not know what Christian eyes look like? Let us hope we do; if not, we must have moved in a very half-hearted Christian environment.

When you or I attempt to rise above the height of our own heads and to conceive the divine glory, our first thought may well be of the infinite scope, the wealth and variety of that all-comprehending life. But what has impressed the great theologians has been the simplicity, the limpid clarity of God.

Our mind is like the eye of an insect, many-faceted; God's mind is like the eye of an eagle, one clear vision of all the visible. We put together with labour the broken aspects of our ideas; he possesses in one sweep whatever is. So, when our little labouring soul gives witness to God, it goes through separate movements of feeling, speech and act. Feeling is blind, speech is insubstantial, act is cold. But the life is the witness, the life in which they all find their place. The life of a saint is his love for God, which is practical, and warm, and expressive; in tongue, in hand, and in heart. It is not conscience, or reason, or obedience, that is the witness to God. Man is the witness, the saint is the witness; and without obedience, without reason, without conscience, he would not be a saint; for without any one of these he would not be a man.

Such is our life, a prism which breaks the single ray of Godhead into partial colours, but such is not God. And where, in the life above all worlds, the Son of God gives answer and testimony to the Father who begets him, there is no difference of heart, hand and tongue. The word which perfectly expresses his understanding is the act of his devotion, which also is the pulse of his being, and the very instinct of his love. He is the faithful witness in heaven, and he is the substance and the bond of our witness on earth, for he unites us with himself in one body by this holy sacrifice.

Preached during Michaelmas Term 1966, as part of a course on the theme: 'Witnesses to God in the Twentieth Century'.

Money

PREACHED IN PUSEY HOUSE
OXFORD 1967

Those wise and good men, the Principal and Librarians of Pusey House, have chalked up 'money' in a list of God's good (but withal dangerous) gifts to us. As they are terribly short of the stuff themselves, they hesitate to speak personally on the dangers attaching to filthy lucre; and they put up a bloated academocrat like the Warden of Keble to preach on their behalf. Well, bloated I may be, but I am still uncertain what it is they want me to preach about. My text is to be that *money* is a good gift of God. But this could mean either of two things. It could mean that a circulating medium of exchange is of vast convenience to mankind in general, or it could mean that it is a personal and individual blessing to be in the money, to have oodles of the stuff, to be a moneyed man. Now the first of these two propositions is indubitable—without a free flow of currency to oil the wheels of exchange, the life of man would be nasty and brutish, and most probably short. But the second proposition is one which a minister of the gospel, however personally bloated, can scarcely be expected to maintain. For is it not written, 'How hardly shall they that have riches enter into the Kingdom of Heaven'? According to the gospel, there is only one blessed thing about wealth, and that is the blessed opportunity to give the blessed lot away—not to hang on to it, and keep patronizing people by letting out little dribs and drabs of it, but to get rid of it at one go, for good and all. Then indeed you will have treasure in heaven. And if you say to me, 'All very fine, but no one acts on that principle, so what's the good of talking about it?' I shall be obliged to contradict you. Christians *do* act on this principle every day: it happens whenever a well-to-do person goes for a monk or a friar, but it happens also in lay life more often than you think. Why, we knew a bachelor don whose books began bringing him in a fortune, so he gave the whole lot away in advance to various charities, tying it all up by forms of law, so that he could not touch a penny of it— a scheme which proved awkward when, years after, he made a late marriage, and had the world's work untying enough of his money to provide for his step-children's bare necessities.

It is good to give riches away—not because money is a bad thing: charity isn't like the hot penny in the children's game, which you pass on as fast as you can from hand to hand, since you are to lose a forfeit if you are caught holding it. No, the reason against holding much money is that money is power, money is opportunity, and your poor neighbours haven't got enough of it. Money is a serious subject. There is nothing more bogus than that affectation of aristocratic high-mindedness which considers the weighing of expenses to be beneath notice, and the paying of tailors' bills to be a bourgeois scruple.

Money is good, say the Principal and Librarians of Pusey House —money is good; but also, money is dangerous—and how right they are! Not merely for the crude reason that one is tempted to collar more of it than one deserves or hang on to more of it than one requires. There are other, more insidious, dangers attaching to a money-governed system, dangers which beset us whether we are moneyed men or not.

First, there are the dangers connected with the fact that money is an accommodation. What I mean is this. If you have to live on a store of food which you have either raised by labour or obtained by barter, and if you have to clothe yourself in what has been spun and woven and cut out and sewn up in your own house, then there is no danger of your living beyond your income. How can you? What you haven't got, you go without. But start living on a bank-balance and you can accommodate things: you can anticipate income, you can borrow it, you can get the Micawberesque feeling that whatever you spend, your money can be stretched somehow, and the day of reckoning postponed. So there springs into being a monstrous pair of Siamese twins, criminal carelessness and sinful anxiety. The thoughtless runner-up of bills begs with shame and agony from his parents, or begs from his college, money which ought to have been available for more necessary uses: or finds himself filling his pocket by doing stupid paid labour when he ought to be getting on with his studies. And what should he have done? He should have worked out what he could afford to spend, and made sure he spent no more. It's a simple duty: do you do it?

Money is, in fact, a disguise. It disguises for us our own position;

it also disguises *from* us the plain fact of our dependence on God and on our fellow men. Our money is something which 'comes' to us: it's my College stipend, it's your educational grant. We do not consider who is paying for us, or why they do it, or what obligations their doing so imposes on us who receive it.

But we can do worse than that. Did I say we *can* do worse? We do. So far from feeling what is done for us as an obligation, we take it as a tribute. The money that is given us shows how people value us: only think of it! I am doing nothing for society, but society thinks me worth so many hundreds a year, because I'm a being of superior intelligence, capable of academic research. We take money to be a value-ticket; we take pay as a yardstick of worth. It is not mere greed that makes a given profession, a given category of workers, clamour for its level of pay to be boosted. It's something even more diabolical than greed—it's worldly pride. Butchers and bakers must keep up their differentials, or people will think them no better than the candlestick-makers. And who would be a parish priest? Parish priests may be paid less than municipal dustmen—Oh, but then their office is divine.—Divine? Come off it, be practical: they're not worth a thousand a year.

This is an ignoble subject: I can't help it—you may blame the Principal and Librarians for that—I must go on dragging you through the bowels of hell. For there's more of it. As we value ourselves on our money, we value everybody else by money, too. It is commonly taken for granted that anyone will change jobs in pursuit of an odd hundred pounds more a year. He'll leave his dear friends behind, he'll uproot his children from their school. Never mind—of course he must go where the money is. Isn't this the *mobility of labour* so dear to the hearts of statesmen and economists? The mercenary vice has three branches: first, go where the money is; second, do nothing except for pay; and third, never refuse money offered. You can get a college, or a university, to accept any substantial benefaction for any object, however distorting to their true aims or aspirations. They just can't bear to turn good money away. Here's a millionaire, or more likely an industrial corporation, ready to endow a professor or build a laboratory for the study of jam-making. Very well, we'll establish an honours school in the subject of making jam. So much for us; and as for you, where is the undergraduate who finds that an extra grant of some kind is available, and who, however little he needs it, does not think how he can qualify to get it?

There is no need to *argue* against the cult of Mammon: it only needs to be exposed. There is no need to *demonstrate* that money is a good servant, but a bad master. The truth is self-evident, and that would be the end of the matter if Mammon were lodged in our heads. Unfortunately it is not so: he is deeply entrenched in our hearts. 'Lay not up for yourself treasure upon earth,' says the voice of Truth himself, 'for where your treasure is, there will your heart be also.' And, 'No man can serve two masters—you cannot serve God and Mammon.' There is only one way to be rid of Mammon-worship, and that is to stop reckoning anything as our own. You cannot serve two masters. If God is the master, everything we have is his; money and the manipulation of money are instrumental to his will.

In the parables of pounds and talents, Christ compares God with a master who entrusted money to his servants, and then called them to account for their management of it. It is commonly supposed that the money of the parable is just a figure of speech. What God essentially requires an account of from us is our use of our gifts and graces: our talents in the metaphorical sense. It is not at all clear to me that this is so—no doubt the parable has a wider application, as wide, indeed, as you can make it—but why should not the first and plainest sense be starkly literal? Will not God call us to account for what we have done with our money? And—one might almost say—the man who can pass that account need be subjected to no other, for what we have done with our money is what we have done with our life. The man who has made an imaginative, a generous, a just, a creative, a living use of his money is a perfect man.

The audit of money is like the audit of time, with which it can be closely compared. Money, as such, is a mere blank; so is time. Time, like money, must be spent, spent wisely, not wickedly or wastefully spent. Of that spending God will surely call us to account. But neither for the account of our time, nor for the account of our money, does God wish us to prepare our ledger by a painful or slavish scrupulosity, counting halfpence and splitting minutes. Where your treasure is, there will your heart be. The heart which makes the love of God and the happiness of men its treasure will spend both time and money well. For the rest, a general vigilance over the use of time and money will suffice.

Christ himself gives us a Franciscan example so far as money is concerned—he left all property behind when he exchanged the carpenter's shop for the field of mission. And as to time—he had, by common expectation, some forty years in hand, when he spent the lot at a single throw, to purchase the pearl of great price, to bring us our salvation. Nothing is ours—indeed, we are not our own—we were bought with a price. Therefore with all we have, and all we are, we are bound to shower forth the praises of our Maker and of our Redeemer.

Preached during Michaelmas Term 1967, as part of a course on the theme: 'Good and Dangerous Gifts'.

Rewards and Punishments

PREACHED IN THE TEMPLE CHURCH LONDON 1962

He shall come to judge the quick and the dead.

How curious nowadays sound those confident appeals to the principle of retribution, which a former generation of preachers made! If God is just, they said, there must be a future life to reward the virtuous, and to punish the wicked. Even granted the principle of retribution, the argument was pushed beyond all limits, in the scope of the rewards and penalties conferred. Whose little virtues deserve everlasting life in the vision of God? And whose vices deserve the gnawing flames of everlasting remorse?

We nowadays punish with regret, and would wish that we need not punish at all. Surely, we say, Almighty Love and Almighty Wisdom can find the way to dispense with so clumsy an expedient. We also feel some qualms about the principle of reward. Why make good men happy? If they are good, they are probably happy already. We would rather make men good by making them happy, than make them happy because they are good. And goodness or no goodness, we should like to make men happy anyhow. That would be worthwhile for its own sake. If they can be good too, why, so much the better.

Moved by reflections such as these, Christians began to wonder whether to believe either in heaven or in hell. For it isn't as though God had immortal souls on his hands, and had got to find a place for them. It now seems obvious that we are not immortal; not, that is, immortal of ourselves. We are only immortal if it pleases God to make us so. We used to say that divine justice would raise us at the last trump to give us our deserts. But if we feel so uncertain about rewards and penalties, we may ask why he should raise us at all?

Those who have to plead causes know how dangerous it is to advance bad arguments. It may be that the case is strong in itself, and has no need of the weak argument with which we support it. Nevertheless, when this quite unnecessary argument is refuted, the case may seem to fall with it. And so it is with future life, and the argument for retribution. The argument was bad, and when it falls, we think that the whole case has fallen. Let us try to put it on its proper basis.

It is undeniable that scripture talks to us of rewards and penalties. But the language of remuneration is not always found pure and unmixed in such connexions. It is commonly blended with ideas of a different sort. A man is said to be paid for his job. But the payment is often said to lie in the success of the job itself. For example, the cultivator is rewarded for his work by the success of his crop. The justice of his master, the landlord, consists in letting him share the produce of his own labour. Such language is quite usual. I would say of students, painfully toiling at the elements of a new tongue, that the *reward* of their efforts would be the mastery of the literature.

Now if people need external bribes, or monetary inducements to do a job, we may accuse them of a mercenary attitude (though we may add in passing, that if we do make such an accusation, we shall indict almost the whole human race). But no one, I think, calls a man mercenary because he wants to make a job of the job itself. He wouldn't be much of a man unless he did. I can tell you, it is a most awful task to write a book, yet the author perseveres because he wants to make a job of it. I dare say he would also like to earn some royalties, but that's a separate consideration.

Now the reward that God promises us is the making a job of our existence, as a Christian understands that existence. What is the job? The job is, to love God and my neighbour; and to get myself in hand, so that I can do it. Well, how far have you got, and how far do you think you will get? Can you even see the God you are trying to love? Sometimes, in a moment of prayer, or in an encounter with surprising goodness, or in the reception of a sudden blessing, you have some sense of God. Such glimpses are precious as foretastes; but if they are not foretastes, they are mockeries. When shall we make a job of the knowledge of God? But we cannot use such language, without its turning completely round in our mouths. We make a job of the knowledge of God, indeed! When will he make a job of uniting us to himself? God cannot be a job for us, we are his job, his handiwork. He can fill us with himself, if he pleases; we shall never come to him, unless he comes to us.

The second part of the job is that I shall love my neighbour.

Ah, when shall love so clear my eyes, that I shall even see one half of what God has put into my neighbour, for me to love?—let alone care for him with the heart of God. Then what heaven, to be in heaven, and see on every side the glory of God reflected in the image of God, which is the human face! What heaven to be in heaven, and to delight, without a barrier, in the company of a thousand friends: when all reserves are down, and all hearts open, and we shall care for the handiwork of God impartially, whether it happens to be in another, or in ourselves!

The third part of the job, and surely the least, is getting ourselves in hand, making ourselves the man we would be. Well, those who are young may hope to make much more progress in this life, but we who have had most of our life, look back and see that we have made little. It may seem an impudent thing if we hope for heaven to do for us what we have failed to do for ourselves; and yet this is the mercy of God, that he does for us what we have failed to do for ourselves. He sent his Son to die for us, while we were yet sinners; every day he renews his forgiveness and his grace. What heaven, then, to be in heaven, to be at one with the will of God, and to go all along with him, as he makes us everything that he desires to make us!

So, then, without heaven we shall never make a job of the job; only we see now that *with* heaven we shall not make a job of it. It is God's job: and he will do it. And his job is all that infinite love suggests to infinite power. He will do all he can for us. And what is that? He will make us perishable creatures to hang on the skirts of his own eternity, and to drink immortal being from the fountain of our creation.

When I turn to what our Saviour said about eternal punishment, I am horrified and abashed; but I do not see myself called to meditate on hell, as I must meditate on heaven. I must think about heaven, because it is the job—it is what makes sense of our present endeavours. The threat of failure is a spur to success, but it is the hoped-for success, not the dreaded failure, that marks out the stages of the work. I must envisage the success; I need merely dread the failure.

Can we say that the sentences of human law cast any light at all on divine punishments? I think we can. Not all legal sentences, perhaps, but some can cast a little light. There is the sort of criminal whose whole life is an imposture. He practises to deceive mankind, and he certainly deceives himself. He is the super-subtle brain, the master-mind, who always gets away with it. Such an imposture must be smashed against the solid rock of moral truth; and one of the ways in which it may be smashed is in collision with the law. So all the rich and the mighty, the heartless oppressors whom scripture consigns to the flames of punishment, are one great and many-headed imposture. Dives's luxurious pride was a living lie; his recompense is the truth of what he was, and of what poor Lazarus was. 'Son,' says Abraham in Christ's parable, 'in thy lifetime thou hadst thy good things, and Lazarus evil things. Now he is comforted, and thou art tormented.'

But, a tender heart will say, is it not still vindictive of God to smash our falsities against the rock of his terrible truth? Why shouldn't he let us go? Let us go? But if our Creator lets us go, we shall undoubtedly perish. Our only life is to be reconciled to him; and we cannot be reconciled to him without being reconciled to truth. That degree of judgement, at least, awaits us all; we have got to see all the lie our life has been. We have got to see what we thought we were, and what we were, we have got to see what God designed us to be, and what we made ourselves to be. We have got to see the scars of our neglect or hardness of heart on our neighbours' souls. We have got to see what a God we have, and how we have used him. That is our purgatory. I do not know if it will be short or long. I am sure it can be shortened hereafter by present penitence. If there are any souls who can never reconcile themselves to God's truth, then in hell they are and in hell they remain.

But we will dare to hope that the very thing that makes our torment will be our joy and our salvation. What is it that will break our hearts, but the vision of the divine mercy which we have disappointed? And what will be our everlasting joy, if it is not that same mercy, full of forgiveness to us and happy to have borne the wounds of our cruelty, if, by bearing them, he can vanquish our enmity?

What is it, then? Our assurance of a life to come cannot be firmer than our assurance of God himself. If you believe that he has saved us, you know that he has saved us with an everlasting salvation; for no salvation that is not everlasting is any salvation at all.

Caprice

Entreat me not to leave thee,
or to turn back from following thee;
for whither thou goest I will go,
and where thou lodgest I will lodge;
thy people shall be my people,
and thy God shall be my God.
Where thou diest will I die,
and there will I be buried.
Let the Lord slay me, and worse,
if aught but death part me and thee.

RUTH 1.16–17

Mothers-in-law have had a bad press on the whole, but Ruth was devoted to hers. That is, whether she was devoted in feeling, I do not know, but on the day when Naomi emigrated Ruth devoted herself to her in fact; and, after that, she was devoted in the literal sense—she had sworn away her liberty, she had committed herself.

I suppose no reader of the book of Ruth has ever blamed Ruth for what she did, or called her a fool; for we all admire people who give themselves away to others, even though we have not the slightest intention of imitating them. Ruth, no less than Orpah, had the chance of freedom in her own country and, if she liked entertaining noble sentiments, splendid opportunities of service, no doubt, to her fellow Moabites awaited her there. It is far from obvious why she should tie an old foreign Jewess round her neck, and drown herself abroad. If she escorted Naomi back to Bethlehem and handed her over to her blood-relations she had done all that was required of her, on the most exacting estimate. Young people should not sacrifice themselves to the old; it's a crime against Youth, is it not? Now Orpah, she was a sensible girl, and she had a heart besides. She cried like anything when she parted with Naomi, and kissed her goodbye in the nicest possible way.

What Ruth did was unnecessary but there is no getting over the fact that this is exactly why we like her. The more casual, quixotic, unnecessary self-devotion is, the more it takes our affections. There is something random, indeed, about all personal devotion. It would be reasonable, I suppose, to be tepidly benevolent to the human race in general, and avoid getting knocked off our base. There's safety in numbers, and the claims of all men upon us are, to a philosophical mind, roughly equal. If we feel equal pulls from all directions we shall not lose our vertical balance. But what do we do? We *fall for* someone, as the saying goes; and often it seems that it might just as well have been for someone else. When did Ruth take the plunge? There in the middle of the path, I fancy, she suddenly knew she wouldn't go back. But if her choice was sudden, it wasn't light or fickle. This girl, if she gave herself, she gave herself. 'Whither thou goest I will go and where thou lodgest I will lodge, thy people shall be my people and thy God my God. The Lord slay me and worse, if aught but death part me and thee.'

'Entreat me not to leave thee.' This at least is admirable in Naomi, that, understanding the passion and the force of the girl she had to do with, she did her best to dissuade. If Ruth, once over the fence, was over and would not go back, it was right to make it as difficult as possible for her to get over in the first place. So Naomi entreated her daughter-in-law to leave her; with her heart in her mouth, doubtless, for fear she might be taken at her word.

And so, we read, Christ deals with his disciples. A scribe—let us say, a don—having offered to become one of his travelling company, Jesus gave him fair warning. 'The foxes have holes and the birds of the air have nests; but the Son of Man hath not where to lay his head.' And on another occasion, when crowds of people began to follow him as he journeyed, 'If any man cometh after me and doth not hate'—renounce, that is—'his own father and mother and wife and children and brethren and sisters, yea and his own life, he cannot be my disciple. Whoever does not take his gallows-tree on his shoulder and come after me, cannot be my disciple.' Therefore, he says, count the cost first, as you would if you were going to build a tower or start a war. My disciples are to be the salt of the earth; but salt with no saltness in it is good for nothing.

So Christ, like Naomi, entreated them to leave him, even though to leave Christ was not merely to let an old woman fend for herself, but to abandon the cause of God. For it has pleased

Almighty God to appeal not only to our reasonable respect, but to our personal devotion, and that he might do this, he has introduced a random and almost irrational streak into the method of our salvation. He comes to us in one particular human person; he appeals to us as Naomi appealed to Ruth. He bids for our hearts in competition with other bidders, and, for fear we should give ourselves, and then regret it, entreats us first to leave him.

Well, but can sheer choice, the attraction of the heart into irrevocable commitment, be the best thing in the world, the key to our paradise? What is the use of disputing about it? We know it is so, with the only sort of knowledge available on such a matter. We know it, even if the world goes against us. And the world does go against us. The society which absorbs us is biassed against personal devotion. It asks us to approve people who conform to a principle called the fluidity of labour; who move freely from one part of the world to another in pursuit of jobs or markets, breaking up personal ties and forming new (if they can be said to form any) as often as they move. For (worldliness holds) men do not need permanent devotions, they want cheerful company, and friendliness will do in place of friends. There remains, of course, the family, so long as it remains—but the general fluidity is infecting it. Ruth's protestation to Naomi sounds like a marriage-vow, but a marriage-vow pronounced with the hearty finality of old-fashioned piety, not with the mental reservations of modern unbelief. If a man does not commit himself to the wife—and indeed the friend— —that he hath seen, how shall he commit himself to the God he hath not seen? It may come about, perhaps, that the call of Christ involves his disciple in 'hating' these natural ties, and transferring to a divine object a loyalty he has learnt on the human plane. But sufficient unto the day is such an agony; and meanwhile, we have no loyalty capable of being transferred to God, unless we practise loyalty towards men.

At this time of the year friends scatter and Christians go out into the world; and it will be seen how many of them have committed themselves to Christ, or to one another. Christ, considered in himself, is the Son of God and the glory of God, and as such we will seek him in our prayer. But Christ as an object of loyalty demands to be accepted in the persons of our fellows. 'Inasmuch as ye did it to the least of these,' he will say to us at the Judgement, 'ye did it to me.' He must be acknowledged especially in his old Naomi, the distressed old woman, the visible Church: often, we think, altogether too old-ladyish a society, and with too many old ladies in it, to start with. But there lies your absolute commitment: if you are committed to Christ, you must not desert that company for so much as a week if you are in reach of it. By your attendance on so simple a duty you will know, and Christ will know, whether you are a disciple or not. We must stand by old Naomi; her people are to be our people, as her God is our God, and nothing but death (we bind ourselves with a curse) is to part her and us.

We must stand by our bond. But our virtue, our devotion, is not the first, nor the principal application of Ruth's example. How we always will insist on beginning from the wrong end, thinking first about ourselves and our virtues, not about God and his love! Is it we that have made the firm, the generous choice of Ruth? 'Lord, I am ready to go with thee both to prison and to death.' 'Peter, I tell thee, the cock shall not crow this day, until thou hast denied me thrice; but I have prayed for thee'—and when will the good will of that prayer be exhausted? He who prays commits himself to Peter not only to the death, but by the death. If there is something always irrational and outside the reckoning about human self-devotion, what shall we say of the act by which the Divine Son descends from the mountains of his glory to meet us on the roads of our migration, making our concern and our life and our flesh and blood his own? His loving-kindness is the Ruth that goes, that goes —where? To the very place where Ruth brought Naomi on her way—for, it says, they came to Bethlehem in the beginning of barley-harvest. Ruth, devoting herself, making herself over, came to Bethlehem, not knowing what part was assigned to her there in the providence of God. She came to Bethlehem, and was received by marriage into the family from whom Jesse and David, and so ultimately Jesus Christ according to the flesh, was born; St Matthew names her among Christ's ancestors. She came to Bethlehem, to take a preparatory and unknowing part in that act of devotion by which the living Love came down and made himself ours everlastingly in flesh and blood that he might make us his.

The Privilege of Challenge

PREACHED IN KEBLE COLLEGE CHAPEL OXFORD 1967

There is a car which I very occasionally see parked opposite the mouth of the den in which I keep my own little monster. But this other car that I speak of . . . only now a horrid thought strikes me. Dare I go on? For it might belong to one of you, and I don't want to be personal. On balance, I think I'll risk it. I don't think it likely that the owner of that car is much of a College Chapel man, or would he have painted it all up in the four primary colours, wildly scrawled; or would he have enriched the effect with mottoes, stating his appreciation of sexual pleasure, his toleration of drug-addiction and his proposal to be free, free, free?

There is no doubt that freedom is in the air, and is the current expression of being adult. You no longer find the glory of growing up in the privilege of herding with the old bucks (and I don't blame you)—you want to strike out a line for yourselves, and though it is depressing to observe how few lines there seem to be, and how many people strike into them, still, it's a noble ambition, is it not? Surely the glory and the responsibility of man is to decide for himself what he will make of his existence. And in this climate of feeling, nothing seems more hopeless than to gain a hearing for talk about *the will of God*. It sounds like sheer fuddy-duddery—the attempt to tie us down by ancestral prescriptions in fixed attitudes, and to deny us the freedom of personal choice. The man who paints up his car like an old canal-barge is admittedly not exercising a very important range of freedom. But for heaven's sake let *us* make up our own minds about what really matters, by the use of such knowledge, judgement, and good feeling as we possess. And let no one dare to say to us, 'God spake all these words and said, Thou shalt . . . thou shalt not . . .' Perhaps we may agree with God here or there—but never mind, don't tell us the answers—it would be like looking up the solution of the crossword in the end of the puzzle-book.

A surprising expression of this mood can be seen in Thomas Altizer's *Gospel of Christian Atheism*, a book which is apparently being read with all solemnity in America and even over here. Altizer's version of the Christian Gospel is that our Creator, realizing the intolerable obstacle opposed by his sovereignty to our freedom, poured himself into a human body so that we could crucify him once for all and be rid of the divine nuisance for ever. I do not think Dr Altizer holds that this is what the New Testament says, but he is very clear that this is what it ought to have said.

I hesitate, myself, to be quite so high-handed with the Word of God, and so I am moved to examine what at certain points it does say. Look, for example, at Christ's parable of the pounds (as St Luke has it) or the talents (as it is according to St Matthew). On the face of it, it looks as though it were going to present a thoroughly servile, anti-freedom sort of moral: for God is presented as a rich slave owner, and men as the slaves whom he holds to a strict account. But when we look closer, we see that once granted the slave-owning model—which was, after all, simply the economic pattern of those times—Christ does everything possible to liberalize it. The master does not indeed hang himself, like the God of Dr Altizer, but he does absent himself, so that his men are left with the maximum of responsibility; and he puts his wealth into their hands. Nor is that all. They are completely free as to the way they choose to set about improving the property—a freedom scarcely enjoyed by the high executives of any great industrial concern today. Without obtaining anyone's agreement or consent, they launch into several branches of trade. If they have not the wit or the enterprise for such endeavour, a mere investment of the money in the enterprises of others will pass muster. They are called to account indeed, and in a sense the account is strict, there is no evading it. But the master is appreciative—he generously praises however much or little they have done; his condemnation is reserved for the man who has done nothing. If their rewards are unequal, it is simply that reward consists in promotion, and they have shown very different degrees of character and competence.

Suppose we ask now, in what manner the freedom of these servants is conditioned by their master's will, during the time of his absence and of their responsibility. May they do anything they think fit? Yes, anything they think fit; but if they are loyal to their position, there are limits to what they can think fit. It is bound to be something that will improve the property, not anything that will spoil it, or that will be simply irrelevant to it. To generalize, we may say that the master's will tells them what's going on, or what business they have to forward—in this case the improvement of a family estate. The rest is up to them.

So much for the parable. And surely everyone who has understood it must admit that it presents a realistic picture of our condition. A thoughtful man is free to do what he thinks fit, but he can't think just anything fit. It will only be fit, if it fits into what's going on— and we cannot force the way of the world into the line we happen to choose. It is no use my deciding to be a Jacobite, and devoting my life to the cause of the Stuart monarchy, because, as the saying is, there's no future in it—and not much of a past in it, either.

The will of God is the Good Old Cause; the cause for which not Charles Stuart, but Jesus Christ, died, and being dead, lives. And it is in the form of God's cause that God's will comes first to bear upon us. It is something to live and die for, something that will employ all our capacity for free endeavour and for wise decision. St Paul called himself the slave of Jesus Christ, and at another time described himself as dragged in triumph at Christ's chariot-wheels. But his life was one of constant decision, knife-edge policy, and endless resource; and why? He had found a motive, a cause, a something, on which to employ his will, to spend, and to be spent.

St Paul was a highly reflective creature, who saw pretty well what was happening to himself, and so it is worth hearing what he has to say about the condition of freedom under the will of God. In fact, he goes on with Christ's story, as we were seeing it in the parable of talents. In 2 Cor. 3.17 we read, 'The Lord is the Spirit; and where the Spirit of the Lord is, there is liberty.' So runs our traditional version. But to understand St Paul, we need to replace 'Lord' by 'Master'—the owner of slaves—and to replace 'liberty' by 'freeman-hood', the status of a free citizen. And then we can see what he is saying: Our Master is the Spirit, that is to say, he is the self-bestowing divine mind. For what do we understand by the name Spirit, but God giving himself; God self-bestowed? And where the Spirit of the Master is, St Paul continues, when it overflows, and shares itself with the servants—there is freeman-hood. They are not slaves, when the mind of the Master is freely open to them, and stirs them with its mighty purposes; they are only slaves, who are ruled by flat commands, in the service of purposes they do not heartily embrace. Where, then, the Spirit of the Master reigns, there is freeman-hood. And we all, with unveiled face, reflecting the glory of the Master, are transfigured into his very likeness from glory to glory, as from the overflowing of the Master Spirit.

Ultimate freedom can in the nature of the case belong to no other will but the Master-will, which wields the world. All other wills are conditioned by the world of which they each form some minute part. But the mastership is not jealously hoarded by the Master, it is imparted to the servants so that they are made sons, partners and friends in that pure and creative freedom, which calls the non-existent into being for the sake of what it can be, and when it has come to be, loves it for the sake of what it is.

Such, according to Christ's Apostle, is the freedom of a Christian man. The divine life broke into our world in Jesus to make us free partners in the Mastership, and by continuing to work in the world, the Spirit of Jesus gives us a cause to live for. Jesus says to his disciples at the Supper, 'You call me Rabbi and Master, and you say rightly, for so I am ... but I no longer call you servants, for the servant has no knowledge of what his master is about. I have named you friends, for all things that I have heard from my Father I have let you know.' And St Paul says to the Corinthians: 'God has revealed his purposes to us through the Spirit, for the Spirit searches all things, even the deep thoughts of God. Who of men knows a man's mind, except the spirit of the man within him? So God's mind none knows, save the Spirit of God. But we have received not the spirit of the world, but the Spirit from God, that we might know the blessed calling bestowed on us by God; things of which we speak not among the pupils of human wisdom, but among the pupils of the Spirit, interpreting the Spiritual to the spiritual. The animal man receives not the teaching of God's Spirit—it is folly to him, he cannot grasp it, for it is spiritually judged. The spiritual man judges all things, and falls under no man's judgement. Scripture says, Who has known the mind of the Lord, to be his counsellor? But we *have* the mind of Christ.'

Privileges are challenges. We have the mind of Christ. Let us turn our thoughts, then, to discovering the work Christ is doing in us and around us, and let us embrace it with a good will. It's our only freedom; it will set our wits and wills abundantly to work.

Radical Piety

PREACHED IN TRINITY COLLEGE CHAPEL OXFORD 1956

Ye trample on the poor and take exactions from him.
AMOS 5.11

The other day a Russian, an ex-communist, came into our drawing-room; and having glanced round at the effects, he summed up the residents, in an aside which was afterwards betrayed to us. 'H'mm, pluto-aristocratic intellectuals.' Aristocratic: that must have been the bits of tarnished Sheffield plate, and of chipped Dresden china, some of which look like, and one or two of which even are heirlooms. Intellectual: the bookcases, I suppose, and a general air of slight discomfort. As to the plutocracy, we may put that down to the somewhat portentous architecture of an official residence.

There I go, you see, laughing it off as best I may; but the impact remains. It is not agreeable to be called a pluto-aristocratic intellectual by a man who has been through the mill in eastern and central Europe. A pluto-aristocratic intellectual may not be so bad as a Fascist hyena, but he is, surely, an unfeeling parasite who plays with letters and forgets the poor. Sometimes, through my pluto-aristocratic windows, there float up angry and amplified revolutionary voices, exerted to attract a crowd in front of St John's College. The tone grates on my intellectualist ears, and I shut the windows. I am a great shutter of windows, but there are some voices which get into the mind itself, and will not be excluded. Voices of famine and despair from men driven by tyranny to revolt, and gone into exile; cries from men, not very numerous indeed, but still they are men, shot by our force putting its strong hand on the Suez Canal.

It would be comforting to throw the blame on the Government: but they—heaven help them!—have been put there to keep the peace. And there never has been a practicable recipe for worldly peace, except the maintenance of the *status quo*. It may be their only course, to maintain it by the measures they have taken; this is not the place to discuss such things. What worries me is the *status quo* itself, a condition of affairs which leaves us pluto-aristocratic intellectuals, or whatever we are, sitting up aloft, and sucking in the riches of the world through channels, or canals, which have to be defended in this kind of way. For it is a sacred duty, by everyone's admission, for the Western nations to defend their standard of living. But I open the Bible, and I find Christ preaching his good news to the poor, and the prophets denouncing the rich. I remember a scholar of St Edmund Hall, whose education had not lain much in the fields of conventional piety, called upon to read a piece of Amos, much like the piece we have just heard. He was a rather theatrical young man, and he gave us the works. His voice broke with passion as he screamed the prophet's indictment of economic tyranny. It sounded for all the world like the oratory in St Giles, against which I shut my windows. The chapel-goers were considerably surprised.

'That was hot stuff', he remarked to me afterwards. 'What on earth was it all about?' I tried to tell him. The rich men in Israel had laid out their capital in financing the farming of their poorer neighbours; and the poor, unable to pay off the obligation in money, had had to pay it in crops, personal service and land. That was all. The poor were reduced to dependence. You might have called it the effect of economic laws; but the prophets called it by other names. They put their finger on the awkward practical point: however it had happened, the rich could set free the poor, and give them back their land, if they liked. And why didn't they? Because they had no knowledge of God. For God is justice, God is mercy.

How simple seems the issue of those days, when we look back upon it! Every rich man a separate tyrant, with his own little empire, which he could liberate if he liked, or if the prophet's sermon got between his ribs. But we pluto-aristocratic intellectuals, or pluto-democratic philistines or whatever we are, have inherited an empire of money power which is a corporate affair of great complexity. No one of us can rush into the street and liquidate it, and if it were suddenly liquidated, there would be great confusion and misery. We are supposed to be in process of liberating our colonial dependants, and meanwhile handing back to them in tangible benefits some return for what we have got out of them. Would the prophet be satisfied with us? And is the God of the prophets satisfied with us as with men who have known him, and bowed the knee before the altar of justice and pity?

Religion, Amos complained, was nothing but a nuisance. Men offered sacrifice instead of making restitution. He would find much of the same folly among us, when prayers for peace and justice are made a substitute for action. There is, besides, a sort of secularized religion—which consists in having a good intellectual and emotional worry about evils we cannot cure; or going through a great business of deciding which attitude we ought to adopt towards them—of which the only visible result is to remove our own mental discomforts. A better sacrifice is money so long as we give enough, and so long as, however much we give, we do not think that that will do.

For it is ourselves we must present. I had a letter the other day from South Africa, deploring the wastage of South Africans who come here to study. They come with noble resolves, but they return neither to teach nor to minister, nor otherwise to make their light to shine: they take the best-paid jobs they can and put their lives into an Anglo-African commercial system which does not look as if it were built to last. And there is nothing singular about the South Africans if they make hay while the sun shines; we all are equally to blame for such materialism.

So, troubled at heart by evils always present, but now breaking out with visible violence, we see ourselves to be too parasitical on the body of mankind, and we ask what we can do. And is not the first answer: 'Look for your true calling, and see whether it has not pleased God to deliver you by drawing you into a way of life which honestly exercised is anyhow not parasitic?' But your vocation is a long-term purpose, whereas the word of God always commands us to act today. What can I do now?

You can work. Work, at least, is not parasitical. You are here to train your powers for all sorts of uses, and while you are making up your minds what their ultimate use shall be, at least you can get on with the training. But if we worked always, we should become very dull. What danger is there of your working always? 'We learn many things in a university beside what study teaches.' No doubt; but those things, I guess, can be trusted to look after themselves. When people say that they learn many things here beside what study teaches, I notice that they never give it as a reason for doing anything they do not like. It is not given as a reason for visiting the infirm, or cultivating the society of the nervous, or coming into the chapel to pray. And yet I suspect that we can learn more from these activities than from getting up plays and going to parties.

Work, like prayer, is the constant object of the devil's attack. He always finds us a plausible reason for doing something else, and so we end up with a prayer which is an apology for not having prayed; and a working record which is an apology against being scolded; and there is a meanness about such a life which it is very unpleasant to contemplate. No one will ever pray, to call it prayer, who does not keep some time inviolable for the purpose, however plausible the devil may be that day with his suggestions of doing something else. And no one will work here as he ought to work who does not keep regular hours for that, hours which only the strongest reason will cause him to break into. It is quite simple, really—it comes to this: either you fit your hobbies in as you can round the solid programme of your work; or you fit your work in round the solid programme of your hobbies. Now which is it? A life of hobbies however cultural will not vindicate us from the accusation, *parasites*.

He that is faithful in little is faithful also in much; and he that has been trusted in small things may be trusted with great. God, who gives you your work to do, and your prayers to say, is testing your fidelity, to see whether you can hold a further trust. You cannot look for a vocation from him if you do not do his will in the first and obvious ways. For those of you who wish to dodge a vocation, here, anyhow, is a useful recipe: waste your time and live without discipline, and you have a fair chance of escaping the knowledge of what God wanted you to have done in the world; he will tell you what it was on the Day of Judgement.

There is a saying of Christ, 'To him that hath shall be given, but from him that hath not shall be taken that he hath.' The sense will be more perspicuous if we remember that 'have' and 'hold' in Greek are the same verb. We put things into hands that can hold them; those that cannot we relieve even of what they do hold. Drop with a crash everything God puts between your fingers, and he will stop putting things there and maybe you will be glad, for the charges God gives about among his servants are not always to their worldly advantage.

And yet—and yet, maybe, we would like to pay off some of our huge indebtedness to mankind, or even—or even our indebtedness to the blood that bought us. Ah, dare I live with the crucifix before my eyes, and dare I die with the crucified to meet—I do not think my regret on that day will be for the opportunities of pleasure I have neglected.

The Transforming Will

PREACHED IN KEBLE COLLEGE CHAPEL OXFORD 1967

We said we would have a course of sermons this term: but as you can easily see by looking at the bill we have pinned up, there is no course about them. The subjects are just an auctioneer's lot—two bedroom chairs, a set of fire-irons, a tricycle and a hen roost. Still some sort of continuity may be recovered, if one preacher actually refers to his predecessor and picks up from there—like beginning with the minutes of the last meeting, always worthwhile if, as the chairman's agenda commonly suggests, there are matters arising from the minutes requiring discussion. And so, for once in a way, we *won't* take the minutes of the previous meeting as read.

Now Mr Pedley* let off a great explosion, and so shook the fabric of the visible Church that one looks round with surprise to see that we still have four walls and a roof here. All forms and fashions, all outward expressions of the Church's presence in the world are bound to change; and most of them are already doomed. It is no use trying to preserve the Church as John Betjeman and his friends aim to preserve a fragment of Victorian Oxford. We shall merely wake up to find ourselves a museum article; or rather, we shan't wake up: for museum articles don't. They are dead and stuffed and pickled in preservative.

Mr Pedley's admonition was necessary, but what's the moral? Are we to withdraw from all established forms of Christian action or observance and do nothing until some transformation of Christian existence has miraculously come about? But in that case, what's the difference between enlightenment and apostasy? If we do nothing we do nothing; we witness to nothing; we annihilate the Church.

When the Archbishop of Canterbury was a young and mischievous man, he and I went into the Chapel at Hawarden Library. I remarked that the crucifix was missing from the altar. 'Yes,' said Michael Ramsey, 'the sub-warden has taken it away. He thinks it is

* At the time, Mr C. R. Pedley was Assistant Chaplain at St Edward's School, Oxford.

more significant to have *nothing* there. He has been reading some German theologians, and he has come to the conclusion that *blank nothing* is the truest symbol of the crucifixion.'

I will not insult your intelligence by explaining the Archbishop's jest. You can see what a remarkably gifted observer would be needed to take note, first, that nothingness was seated in the place of the crucifix; and second, that it was intended as a symbol of what it didn't replace.

Michael Ramsey's remark was a jest, but by no means an idle jest. *Nothing* witnesses to *nothing*. We can't witness to the purity or contemporaneity or adaptability of the Gospel by detaching ourselves from every positive expression of its message and we can't witness to the freedom of Christ's presence in our midst by deserting those hidebound ceremonies, the sacraments. We shall only find out how the Gospel message needs re-wording by preaching it with passion in the form in which we know it for true. We shall only achieve a more effective sacramentalism by throwing ourselves into the observance of the sacraments as we have them, and grasping the substance beneath the forms. As Mr Pedley said, we must put our confidence in *truth*. But that doesn't mean sitting back, and waiting for the truth to shine from above, as one might sit back and wait for the day to break. It means following with devoted obedience the truth *we have seen* as true, with an entire confidence in God, that he will correct, clear and redirect our vision, to the perception of a freer and a deeper truth. Go with the truth you have, and let it carry you into collision with the hard rocks of fact, and then you'll learn something.

So, I'm sure, Mr Pedley meant: but I wonder what, in my stupid youth, I'd have made of it if I had heard him then? For there I was, as are some of you, considering a vocation to Holy Orders. And how would I have reacted? Should I have said: 'Dear me, I'd better think twice before I commit myself to anything so antiquated as the ecclesiastical machine'? Or should I have said: 'Goodness, there never was a time, then, when Christ had more use for a devoted and well-equipped band of apostolic ministers, ready for any change of function or of circumstance they may have to undergo.' If I had taken Mr Pedley's message in this second sense, and taken it to heart, I might have proved a more useful and a more adventurous man than I have. I might, moreover, have suffered less dismay from some of the things that happened to me in my early ministerial attempts. But if I had taken him in the other sense, then perhaps I should have wholly marred a calling with which God had called me.

Is there a feeling of spiritual revolution in the air of England today? No doubt; but no greater, surely, than the sense of spiritual revolution in Palestine when Christ walked the earth. If you think that the Church in its inherited and medieval form is now done for, how much more was the Jewish Church then apparently done for! For the Church of Jewry was a nation, a free and godly kingdom, and now their natural existence was once for all finished. The seemingly timeless dominion of the eternal city had overtaken them: and Israel was wax in the hands of Rome.

What, then, did Jesus do? Did he sit still and wait for a spiritual revolution to occur? Or did he sit down and work out a new and speculative spiritual system, adapted to Roman imperial conditions? He did neither. He gave an absolute form to the religion which he and his people had; and then he threw it hard against the cruel facts. Israel was a nation, a kingdom. Very well, here am I, he said, risen up in the place of my ancestor David, to be your king. Never mind that it doesn't fit—that Caesar is on the throne, and Herod is his puppet. I have come to you so that, rallying round me, you may be the kingdom of God on earth; for the rest, we will put it into the hands of God to do what he will with the world and with us. The clash was inevitable: Jesus's kingdom collided with the priesthood of Caiaphas and the Empire of Caesar. He was crucified; and a new religion, liberated from racial bonds, sprang alive from the Easter sepulchre to conquer the world.

The words and the deeds of Jesus must never be separated from one another, for Jesus, word and deed, was all of one piece. Whatsoever you ask, he said to his disciples, it shall be done for you! That is what he said. But then look what he did—he prayed for present escape from his passion in Gethsemane, and he didn't get it—and how reasonable so to pray, not only for his own sake, but for the sake of the cause! How unprepared his followers were for the ordeal that awaited them! Surely a year's respite—six months' respite—would be infinitely worth while. Yet as he prayed, he saw he could not pray that prayer, and he bowed to his Father's will. Did his prayer go ungranted, then? No, certainly it was granted. For Jesus was doing his best to pray for the triumph of God's saving will, and God more effectively and more immediately achieved the victory of his cause, precisely through his defeat and death.

More than all we ask for will be granted, if two conditions are present: first, a passionate concern for what we conceive the will of God to be; and second, an entire submission to the will of God, as God actually means it to be. How hard it is, to be strongly concerned for the will of God as we think we know it; and yet so detached from our conception of it, that we rejoice to have our purpose transformed by the overruling of God's hand! It may be hard, but it is this concern, and this detachment, this assertion of purpose, and this submission, that once made Christianity out of Judaism, and that has constantly transformed the Church from age to age.

Ask whatever you will, and it shall be done . . . So it is said to me. But shall I demand that the promise should hold good for me otherwise than as it held good for Christ himself? Christ's prayer could not fail, because what he desired was the triumph of the Supreme God, which is the will of God for us. The fact that his prayer became perfect only in the process of praying and of living —what was that? Something hardly worth mentioning. Why trouble to talk about the mental moves through which his will was daily united with the Almighty Love? The union took effect and that was all.

We must pray, for prayer is neither more nor less than living with God. Shall I live today of myself and by myself, or shall I live it with God? Doubtless, whether or not I live it with God, God lives it with me—but that only makes it the more monstrous that I should not live it with him. Prayer is just living with God: looking at him, regarding his will, reaching out our hands for the blessings he is so eager to give, bringing our action into his. We must pray. If you cannot pray, come and ask for help. What could be more natural, than for a Christian to say to a priest, may I make a date to talk to you about my prayers? What else are we for?

Living Tutors

PREACHED IN KEBLE COLLEGE CHAPEL
OXFORD 1963

When I was a freshman to this College—dear me, it's three years ago, and it seems like yesterday—a lot of things happened which surprised me. For instance, on the Thursday before term I was sitting in my study, when suddenly a hundred men whom I had never seen in my life presented themselves. They said they had been told to call upon me; indeed, what was most perplexing of all, they said that I had told them to do it. We had a sort of extemporized and ragged party, which lasted most of the day. Well, I got them all into my study, and through my study, and out of it again somehow. Since then we have got the introductory ceremonies somewhat more under control, but I can't feel that the essentials of the situation have been materially altered. There was something deeply symbolical about that experience of being rolled over by a wave of one hundred men, and of being quite unprepared.

What ought we to do with our wave of a hundred men? Sort you out quickly into Christians and unbelievers; channel the Christians into a regular pattern of Christian life, and organise them into a force which will convert the non-Christians? No doubt, but while we are forming these admirable plans of action, the great wave has rolled over us and scattered itself all over the shore. In a few days you are completely out of control. You begin moving about with a bewildering rapidity; you grow and you shave off beards. A man who said he was a Christian yesterday professes unbelief today: and why? You have met a humanist and like his (or more probably, her) face. This radiant being does not believe in God. You feel ridiculous, and what you thought meant everything to you, your religion, suddenly means nothing to you at all. It isn't done, or it isn't contemporary, or it isn't clever, to believe in God. That's final.

Anyhow, one thing is clear. The pastoral efforts of that well-meaning minority, the Christian dons, aren't worth revolting against. We are completely powerless: as powerless as—as powerless as Jesus Christ, according to the chapter of St Matthew that has been read to us. To go a few verses back in chapter 11, Jesus says of his Jewish audience, that they are like children who won't play: John Baptist wailed to them, and they would not lament; Jesus pipes to them and they won't dance. You might think, he continues, that wisdom would be accepted on the evidence of her works. But no, though Christ has healed the body and the soul, Chorazin is unimpressed, Bethsaida and Capernaum are unrepentant.

So what? At that season Jesus broke out and said, 'I thank thee, Father, Lord of heaven and earth, that thou hast hid these things from the wise and prudent, and hast revealed them unto babes; yea, Father, for that it was well pleasing in thy sight.'

Why, we might ask, does he thank God for so unsatisfactory a state of affairs? No doubt everything God does is ultimately for the best and the pious man will try to praise him for everything however apparently bad—as, in the burial-service, the mourners are made to thank God for taking their friends away. The other day I was present in a committee who were trying to redraft that prayer, and make it sound less unconvincing. I can tell you we found it a difficult exercise.

But it is not in any such spirit of sad and passive acceptance that Christ thanks the Father for his mysterious ways with the children of men. No, it is because the divine gift to mankind is such a marvellous thing, that it has to be like this. For what is the secret? It is, that no one knoweth the Son, but the Father, and no one knoweth the Father, but the Son. If God is not our Father, then he is nothing to us. But the fatherhood of God is not a theory of what the world in general, and human life in particular, looks like from outside. Take the fatherhood of God, and try it on the scheme of things, and you will be landed in the same agonies and absurdities as poor Job was, whenever he tried to square his misery with the principles of divine benevolence. You had a specimen of that in the first lesson. No, Christ does not preach a theory of the fatherhood of God applicable to the general face of things. He says you can get behind the face of things, and back to the heart of things, by living in sonship to God. So far (if you like a bit of jargon) Christ is an existentialist. The quality and the root of existence are uncovered by those who venture to live, and the truth is in the living. No one can do it for you; you have to do it for yourself. No one can convince you with a theory, and if you like to say that all theologies are dead idolatries of the mind, well, in a sense, so they are. No one can find the fatherly heart of God but the son whom God brings into relationship with himself. And until you have found that middle point, the theology makes little sense, if any.

Christ, then, is a sort of existentialist. Existence is plumbed to the bottom by actually existing, and by facing what comes and running away from nothing, by taking fair decisions in impossible situations; and the final lesson is not learnt, except by facing death. Your life is your laboratory, and you are your own experimental material.

A sort of existentialism—but not the solitary sort. Being a son to God, and having God for a father, is to tread, after all, a path that has been trodden; and Jesus, who knows what he is, proposes himself for a guide. 'None knoweth the Father save the Son, and he to whom the Son pleases to reveal him. Come unto me, all ye that labour and are heavy laden, and I will give you rest. Take my yoke upon you, and learn of me, for I am gentle and lowly of heart, and ye shall find rest for your souls. For my yoke is kindly and my burden light.'

When Jesus said this, he was quoting Jesus—there were so many who had had his name before him, and it is natural enough that he should have valued the inheritance. There was Jesus, the old don, the son of Sirach, whom we call Ecclesiasticus. And this is what he had put into his school prospectus: 'Draw near unto me, ye unlearned, and lodge in the house of instruction . . . Put your neck under the yoke, and let your mind receive learning: it is close at hand for you to find. See with your own eyes how I worked but a little, and found for myself much rest.'

I do not see how it can be doubted that the words of Jesus Christ are meant to echo the words of Jesus, son of Sirach. And so it is plain that Christ offers himself to us as a tutor. We know that we can get nothing out of a tutor, unless we accept the yoke, that is, put on the harness. It may be that there are many better paths of study, and wiser systems than the one your tutor offers, but if he is worth having at all, you must discipline yourself and work his way; must be patient of what seems unamusing; must read the books, attend the classes, write the essays.

So Jesus asks us to try his way; and who can consider it, without seeing that there is a depth of truth in it, the truth of life itself? Like a tutor, he asks us to be patient, in learning and in following his ways. But he is not a tutor in mere learning, he is a tutor in living; or rather, a tutor in sonship to God. And sonship to God is not passive obedience. The sonship of Christ is adult sonship—the Son shares his Father's mind, and has his Father for his friend.

According to the words of Christ, revelation begins with the Father's knowledge of the Son. The Father knows who the true Son is, and what he is, and the Father makes us recognize it. That is, God himself moves us to see that Christ is Christ. Next comes the Son's knowledge of the Father: those who recognize Christ, and take his yoke upon them—who put themselves to school with him—they find the fatherly heart, and the liberating will, of God.

And so it lies with God, and with you—and not, or scarcely at all, with us—to make your time here a double school, not only of learning, but of living. We pray that you may find that pearl of price, to buy which, a man should give all he has; and for ourselves we pray, that we may learn along with you, and not heap obstacles in your path.

Consecrated Bread

PREACHED IN PUSEY HOUSE OXFORD 1960

The scientific history of words tends to be disappointing. How many distributors of school prizes have gone to town on the noble assertion that education is a drawing-out, not a putting-in! Historically speaking they are wrong. Education is just a raising or a bringing-up. Take another case—our family name. We were solemnly told by our uncles that a farrer was a farrier or *ferrarius*: to wit, a blacksmith, a fine, muscular fellow. Alas, nothing of the sort: the Farrers were nothing more interesting than fair-hairs, Danish lads infesting Northumbrian shores; not blacksmiths in fact, but whiteheads. Or there's the word 'university': a glorious idea, *universitas studiorum*, the whole gamut of faculties, all the things there are to know! That's not a university, we say of some one-eyed place: it gives degrees in nothing but business economics. As usual, history lets us down: it wasn't *universitas studiorum*, the whole gamut of studies, which gave us the word, it was nothing more interesting than *universitas studentium*, the whole body of students in a given place, say Paris or Padua. Never mind, you may say, to hell with etymology; the false derivation gives us a true and beautiful idea. The whole round of the universe of knowledge, or at least, of enquiry, that's the university: everything from Egyptology to nuclear physics, from pitch-and-toss to manslaughter. Our Senior Tutors, woe to their souls, channel us into lines which suit the teaching staff, and they treat us as tutorial fodder, not as hungry minds. But that's simply an abuse; once we are in the university, we have the right to satisfy our intellectual cravings. So what shall it be? What shall we take? In all this university, this universe of enquiries, what shall I take? John is taking Law. I shall take French and German. Goodness! I hope I'll get through the prelim.

And there's another thing. Suppose I do take what I like, and manage the job, what about all the other subjects of knowledge which by my specialization I neglect? Well, it can't be helped; one can't attend to everything in a limited time. The great thing is, to get some foothold on the continent of exact and disciplined thought; one can always branch out from there in any required direction. Surely a man who's read Plato and Aristotle can master the directions for working a sewing machine. So, reinforced by these comforting considerations, you look at the universe of enquiry, and you decide what you will take.

As you like to look at it, the choice seems either portentous, or trivial. If you take your studies seriously, you set a lifelong direction to your mental interest by the choice of the school you take; but then again, you have, perhaps, no very solid grounds for taking one before another: you are moved by a detestation of Anglo-Saxon, or a desire to be different from your elder brother. Your choice is not like the choice of God, when he decided what he would take. He also looked out upon and surveyed a *universitas*, a universe of wise and perfect thoughts, his own; but these thoughts of his, unlike the strengthless insubstantial thoughts of men, had embodied themselves in solid shapes and living creations, they had become a world. The Creator's thoughts are actual creations; because he thinks us, we exist. And in this universe of his substantial thought, God chose what he would take, and bind himself to, for ever; one line, one lot, one portion of creaturely existence. For at all costs he was determined that he would gain a foothold on the continent, our continent of human life.

If he was to do so, how narrow was the choice! God was to be man, then he was to be one man in all the million million first and last created; so he took flesh, flesh from a Jewish girl, and he became a certain carpenter in one small Galilean town among many, and in one year among all the yearly cycles of the revolving sun. Yet he had no intention of remaining shut up in the lot of life he had taken; once he had taken it, he could branch out from there. There were, there are, no limits to the distances he could reach from that base, the fields of life he could embrace and could annex; until he should encompass the *universitas hominum*, the whole body of men who walk this earth, or fly this atmosphere.

He took flesh, it was his body; it cried and smiled and sucked, it hungered and thirsted, it laboured and grew weary, it suffered and rejoiced, it lived and died. But before it died, before he died as bodily man, he also took bread, and said *it* was his body.

Well, in a manner of speaking, the bread he took *was* his body.

A sculptor might show you round his shop, and pointing out pieces of wood grained suitably for several purposes, might say, 'That is a Churchill, and that's a Victory: that is a greyhound, and this is a leopard.' They are the raw materials of these things; and the food we will eat is the raw material of our body; let us call it our body if we like, by anticipation, or by exaggeration. Yet the bread Jesus took was not his own loaf or roll, that he would eat. It was the bread of the grace, a loaf specially symbolical of the whole company's food: a loaf over which grace was said for them all, and of which everyone present must taste a crumb. It did not stand for the bread or body of any one person there present, it stood for the common food of them all. As St Paul says, writing of this very matter, because the loaf is one, we many are one body, for we all partake of the one loaf. Since food becomes our body, eating from one loaf or from one dish becomes a sort of natural sacrament. As we build up our body from one stock, we feel ourselves tied together in one body corporate; we are members one of another. And to the Jew, this natural tie became a religious bond: the one loaf shared by all was consecrated through the thanksgiving, or grace-before-meat.

This, then, was the bread Jesus took, on the night before he suffered, the bread which was the body of them all; it was this he called his body. The body he took from Mary was no one's but his. From the moment of birth it ceased to be hers; and it was certainly no other man's or woman's. But the bread he took to be his body was the body of the company, of Peter, John, James, Matthew and Thomas: so determined he was, that the effect of his incarnation should not be shut within the confines of his skin. He took their body, but he took it to be made his own, to be consecrated, divinized, Christed; through the oblation of a voluntary death, and the power of a glorious resurrection.

Who supplied the bread which lay on the table at Christ's last earthly supper, and which he took, and held in his blessed hands? We cannot be certain. We hear something of the householder who so providentially and surprisingly offered them a supper-room; we cannot suppose that he also laid on the supper. Judas held a purse, from which the common expenses of the brotherhood were defrayed: perhaps it is right to think that purse purchased the bread. If so, the bread and the body were theirs, were the whole company's, not merely in the sense that the bread was appointed for their use, to be the common substance of their bodies; it was theirs in the further sense, that it belonged to them by purchase and possession; their hands set it on the table. However it may have been with Christ and his disciples, it is at least clear how the case was with St Paul and his friends, say those at Corinth. The materials of the holy feast were neither supplied by the hospitality of a rich householder, nor were they purchased out of a common Church fund. They were brought by the congregation. Every man brought his piece of bread, his little cup or flask; but they were not (it was here that St Paul rebuked them)—they were not each man to eat and drink his own. All was to go into the common stock and be equally shared, after one loaf, picked at random, had been blessed by the bishop and the crumbs passed round; and so likewise with the cup. The remainder would be for the poor.

Christ takes; it is our privilege to bring. Christ takes, through the hands of the priest his representative; we bring the token and stuff of our bodies, no longer in bread and wine, but in the money of the offering, for which the bread and wine have come to be exchanged. It is easily said, that the substitution is bogus; that to give money is one thing, to give ourselves is another. The objection is only valid, if the giving costs us nothing. The only absolute way for us to give ourselves, is as Christ gave himself, in a voluntary death; there is no part of the person left out of such an offering, and we shall all have to make it in some fashion, grudgingly or willingly, when we come to die. Short of that, we can give ourselves only in giving what is ours: our attention, our effort, our sympathy, our patience, our money, our time. Believe me, you are more likely to make a real offering of yourself to God by a decent and costly alms; a bit of your heart will stick to the precious coin, and come away with it, for where thy treasure is, there will thy heart be also—I say that you will probably make a more genuine self-offering in hard cash than by eloquent and invisible acts of the spirit in which you aspire to give God everything—that is to say, to give him what you will take back from him half an hour after: as Peter did, for all his fine words, when he denied Christ in Caiaphas's court.

Dear me, what we give to God isn't much, and our giving isn't much of a giving; so let's be thankful that your preacher is not put up here to discourse on so depressing a theme. No; it is not my text that they gave or presented the bread of the offering (about which, as we have seen, the Evangelists are silent) but that Christ took it into his blessed hands, and said it was his body. He took, and he takes. He takes what we are: he is not ashamed of us, does not discuss us. Peter might deny Christ, but Christ set his eyes on Peter, his eyes and his heart. He takes us, and says we are his body; for his love will make us so. We read of the great St Bernard, that he took some strange monks into his monastery, confident, and rightly, that the love of God in their Abbot's bosom would make Christians of them. But he was only the instrument and copy of his Redeemer. He takes us: he loves us for what we are, and loves us into what we must be; he takes us, incorporate with him through his death and resurrection, and gives us back ourself, that is himself, in the communion of bread and wine.

Now therefore to the living love of Heaven, Creator and Saviour of all, who most wonderfully ordained the excellence of man's estate, and more wonderfully has redeemed it, One God in three Persons, Father, Son and Holy Ghost, be ascribed as is most justly due, all might, dominion, majesty and power, henceforth and for ever.

Preached during Michaelmas Term 1960, as part of a course on the theme: 'Holy Eucharist'.

Pruning for Perfection

PREACHED IN KEBLE COLLEGE CHAPEL
OXFORD 1964

I still get official letters addressed to my predecessors. No doubt it is with a touch of annoyance that my correspondents become aware of their mistake. 'Well,' says the secretary to her boss, 'need we trouble to acknowledge Dr Farrer's letter?' 'Farrer? who is he?', says the boss. 'Oh, he's the man who isn't really Abbott.' To be thought even the shadowiest substitute for the Dean of Westminster should be fame enough for any reasonable man: and yet, such is vanity, I'd rather be known as myself, than as the man who isn't Abbott.

Poor Matthias, unlucky saint! We shall always think of you as the man who isn't Judas; there is no other circumstance of your life, good or bad, on record, except your having been substituted for that apostate soul. Twice in seven years you get a Sunday evensong: but how are we to preach about your merits?

One could preach, indeed, for several hours on the significance of Matthias's election: the fact that, when one of the twelve went to hell (as they supposed) his colleagues found another in his place; whereas, when one of them went to heaven by the most sure road of martyrdom, they did not dream of replacing him. Here is much food for thought. Evidently, to start with, heaven and earth were all one thing to those heaven-centred minds. The Church, the Israel of God, must be complete, an army brigaded, like the old Israel, under twelve patriarchs or princes. When Christ chose twelve disciples, he did not act by chance; he was making it plain for all to see, that God's twelvefold Israel was being rebuilt on new foundations. The twelve foundations, the twelve apostles, must remain. If one fell into the abyss, he must be replaced; if one was raised to glory, he was all the more confirmed in his apostleship: for he was with Christ, and Christ was the very heart and substance of the Church, whether on earth or in heaven.

So the good apostles, dead or alive, were still with their friends: they held the spiritual thrones which Jesus had promised them, to reign with him over the twelve tribes of Israel. If they vanished from mortal sight they needed no successors, but only deputies, such deputies as the sovereign leaves in London when she goes abroad. The first apostle to die was St James, the brother of St John, and it must have seemed a special providence to simple faith, when another James, the brother of the Lord, was ready to carry on in his name. Jesus had made three disciples—Peter, James and John—the privileged witnesses of his glory. A score of years later, when St Paul came to Jerusalem to check his gospel against the authentic tradition, James, Peter and John were still accounted the three pillars of the truth; it was another James, indeed, but what of that? James was simply James.

So the Church is an everlasting but growing force: her apostolic ministry rooted in heaven, branches out through history and bears its sacramental fruit. There is no need to be frightened by the expanse of time, so long as life has the vigour to span it. I suppose there are oak trees standing now whose grandmother oaks had taken root before Christ was born; the apostolic tree, planted in Christ, makes of all history her own biography.

Jesus at the Supper, commenting on the fall of Judas, speaks of the branching tree, the fruitful vine, made all the more fruitful by the lopping of unprofitable boughs. Even those that are spared by the vine-grower's hand, need pruning. What principle does the pruner follow, as he makes his quick immediate practised judgements, moving his knife from twig to twig? May we not say that he spares the growth which can draw effectively on the fruit-bearing vitality of the stock? Poor silly vine, she is sadly inclined to dissipate her energies: she can't help branching out in every direction where there promises to be the slightest scope for her growth. So she wastes her strength on unprofitable ventures; she gets in her own light, she tries so many branches half-heartedly that she achieves nothing thoroughly.

Here, anyhow, is a Lenten lesson, if ever there was one. Do you want to bear fruit for God? Then simplify your life: do fewer things, and do them better. Your instinct is to throw branches in all directions—to try everything. Was there ever such a spectacle of divided energy as the life this university presents? You are all going to be actors, journalists, politicians, athletes, artists, musicians; you are all going to come to the top in study, social influence, wit, taste, friendship and love. Well, if we didn't try everything, we should not know what to drop; if the vine didn't shoot vigorously in all directions, the pruner's knife would lack material to shape a perfect tree. Still you must prune, or you bring no fruit to perfection.

Fundamental to the Christian's pruning is the thought that he must be true to the stock of his vine, he must not degenerate from Christ; he must keep a controlled pattern of activity, such as the fruitbearing vitality of Christ can invigorate. Well, but how do I know, among all the innocent and agreeable things there are to occupy my time, which Christ approves best? I may often be genuinely uncertain; but there is at least one plain principle to guide my pruning. I do know there are certain branches of activity which belong to him: my prayers, my worship, my work; and all acts of charitable kindness. I ought to prune what interferes with these things: the selfish pursuits which make me forget, or put off, kindness to any depressed, sick, or less successful friends; the self-indulgent nights, which make me unfit for the communion I had meant to make in the morning; the trivial book which kept me from writing to an affectionate parent—but I am sure I need not go on and on with such suggestions: surely you know where you ought to prune.

Pruning has highly positive results, but in itself it's a negative thing. Our Saviour has more positive things to say. Not only, he says, submit to God the Father's pruning knife; but also, and still more, abide in me: in me, the stock of the vine. Abide in me, he says, and then, a little later, abide in my friendship, or love. And how? By doing my bidding, he says.

What? after all this talk about mystical union, and loving friendship, does it come down to this? Is it flat obedience after all, the keeping of rules? It is not. Jesus is talking about love, friendship, kindness: let's fix our eyes on that. Friendship, friends: how maddening they can be! Oh, heaven deliver me from the clever friend who never does what I want, but always something much better he has thought of himself! I am going to keep a date somewhere: may I take a snack with him? No, it won't do, it has to be a special meal in some restaurant which takes hours and hours. He's going into town, will he bring me a bit of deal for a carpentry job? Oh, no, he has to bring me a new patent hardboard which he has decided is far better. Will he ask so-and-so to exchange his appointment with mine? No, he thinks how much more suitable it would be to ask somebody else.

How can friendship survive a continual course of such behaviour? If you do what I say, you will stay friends with me. It isn't (I trust) that I want to call the tune the whole time. Mutual complaisance is the rule in friendship, as in marriage: each shall have his turn. And of course, we have had our turn: the saviour of the world has carried the can for us.

So, 'Do what I say and you will abide in my love' has an obvious human sense, let alone a divine. But the divine sense goes deeper. For when I ask my friends, or without asking just expect them to be compliant with my wishes, the wishes are mostly concerned with my affairs, not with theirs. Not all my wishes, I hope, are culpably selfish, but they are mostly personal. But Christ's wishes are nothing but his friendship, or kindness for us. He wants us to be splendid and fruitful creatures, a blessing to ourselves and to one another. So, 'Do my bidding and abide in my love' has a special force. His bidding *is* his love. By doing his bidding, we swim with the very current of his kindness to us. We draw from the stock of the vine that very sap which vitalizes the branches.

Alas, poor Judas, we do not know by what degrees of falling away he slipped out of that kindness of Christ which it is life to have. But let *us* look for his good pleasure, and follow his kind bidding when it is most plain: so shall we be his disciples, and so shall we bear much fruit.

Preached on the Eve of St Matthias, which in 1964 was the Second Sunday in Lent.

Fences and Friends

PREACHED IN ST PAUL'S CATHEDRAL LONDON 1958

> Ignoring God's righteousness,
> and setting out to establish their own righteousness,
> they have not submitted to the righteousness of God.
>
> ROM. 10.3

I cannot preach to you about St Paul's School—it isn't a subject—but I can preach to you about our glorious patron, the Apostle of Christ. May the prayers of that fervent and tireless heart be poured for us on high. What a man, but first of all, what a fact! Who could have hoped, on grounds of general probability, that within twenty years of Christ's resurrection, a man of first-rate genius, a contemporary of Christ himself, would begin a series of letters, breathing the very life and spirit of the new faith; and that those letters should have been preserved! It is astonishing how people nowadays imagine that the evidence of Christianity rests on the gospels, nameless compilations of second-hand witnesses, rather than on the unimpeachable authenticity of St Paul. It is because the gospels fill out the sort of picture St Paul sketches, that we ought to believe the gospels.

The first importance of St Paul, then, is simply that of the articulate apostle, whose testimony we have. All the apostles testified; but Paul wrote. He debates with his fellow-apostles, but under the differences of policy we can see the agreed basis of belief. St Paul and St Peter fought, but they did not fight about the creed.

On a day when we are to praise St Paul, however, we want to think not of what was common, but of what was personal: about that aspect of truth which was specially dear to our apostle's heart, and for which he strenuously contended: justification by faith.

When St Paul preaches justification by faith, one of the things he is doing is what we have all done—he is reacting against the stuff he was brought up on. When he was a boy in the synagogue, this is the sort of thing he was subjected to. 'My dear brethren', said the good old Rabbi, 'the Holy One—Blessed be he!—has longed for your salvation since the foundation of the world. What then, has he done to secure you for himself? He has not left you floundering in the waters, he has thrown you a rope, he has let down a ladder to you.' (Here the Rabbi went off on to Jacob's ladder for about twenty minutes: we will leave that bit out.) 'And what,' said he, returning to the point, 'is the ladder? It is The Commandments. The Holy One has said to you: keep the commandments, and I will admit you to the paradise from which I cast Adam out' (then ten minutes or so on Adam and Eve). 'Not, my brethren,' continued the Rabbi, 'that you really deserve paradise for doing the commandments of God. You are like children, whom their father allows to earn a treat or a prize by doing little tasks which he could himself do in less time than it takes him to explain them to his boys. It is all of love that the tasks are assigned. Light is the labour, and everlasting is the reward.'

Such was the doctrine of the Jewish preachers, and the gist of it was this: God has given you certain limited tasks laid down in his commandments, and it's up to you to do them. You can do them, and if you do them it is God's loving pleasure to reward you with everlasting life. As you can see, it was an amiable doctrine, a humane doctrine, and a doctrine which gave men a motive to exert their wills. What made St Paul so bitter about it? Well, what do you think of it yourself? Just a bit too cosy, wouldn't you say—a doctrine of limited liabilities, a doctrine for the engravers of laudatory tombstones in the eighteenth-century style, or for the writers of appreciative little obituary notices in the columns of *The Times*. We assume that the person to be praised had an area of duty sketched out for him by destiny, and that he cultivated it with distinction. A decent son and, when he married, exemplary in his own household, sound in his comfortable and well-paid profession, delightful in his circle of friends. A nice little four-field farm of duty, you see, had been hedged in for him by fortune—sonship, parenthood, friendship, profession—and not a field of the farm neglected: it would be unreasonable to have asked the man to go outside the hedges. By Jove, though, he did—he took in another field, quite voluntarily—he became an expert on tropical fish, and the regional aquarium is much indebted to his advice.

It is a cosy conception of life, and enables us to take a comfortable view of comfortable men. I suppose that, of all the periods in my own life when I look back upon it, the one which fitted the scheme best was the last years at school, and the years of under-graduate study. It was delightful being an exemplary student, especially when one's friends were so nice, and when one had a taste for academic study, and a still more pronounced taste for academic success. Among the other pleasures there was the pleasure of personal comparison—the pleasure of amiably pitying that foolish fellow Philip (as I will call him though that was not his name): so clever, so idle, so amusing, so appreciative of myself, and doing absolutely no good, no good at all, poor chap; playing bridge all night, drinking too much, getting into a rather queer state, really. But wasn't I supposed to be a Christian, and shouldn't I show him a better way of life? It seemed so awkward, and so boring—another day, perhaps. When he went down, Philip wasn't easy to place. He tried a job, hated it, threw it up, was said to be skulking at home, getting queerer and queerer. I went to see him, and we played chess, played chess and staved off conversation.

'Really,' I said, as I came away in the train, 'Philip is getting queer! I'll propose a joint holiday this summer—perhaps the cheering effect of my wholesome company for a fortnight or so . . .' Then a month or two after the game of chess, at some sort of college reunion, my neighbour said to me, 'Philip—now there was a clever chap; he could have done it! If only he hadn't gone and put his head in the gas oven!' I dropped my spoon in my soup. 'Oh, I say! Didn't you know? I'm sorry (said my neighbour) if I've spoilt your dinner.'—'Oh, good heavens,' I said, 'one can always eat.'

Well, God wanted me, I suppose, to be a dutiful student, but he had also said to me, thou shalt love thy neighbour as thyself, and Jesus said there were no little hedges to be put up between who is my neighbour, and who isn't; and in any case, Philip was inside the hedges, surely. I could try to make the hedge run *half*-way across Philip himself—Philip the cheerful acquaintance, Philip the fellow-scholar, was inside my hedge; but Philip the immortal soul, Philip the hopeful citizen of this world and the next—he belonged to his parents, or to the College chaplain (what a hope!), but anyhow not to me. It was an attractive line of thought, but it didn't somehow convince. Didn't someone once say, 'Am I my brother's keeper?'

So there are all the hedges round our neat garden-plots of duty broken down and yawning open. On the one side the awful gulf of human need, and on the other side the no less awful gulf of the life of God. If I could stretch up and explore that immensity of God, and learn to live in the air of God's Spirit, then, perhaps, I might be able to do something to fill that other gulf of human need, the emptiness of the soul. Poor Philip, he had a characteristic trick. By not sleeping, taking no exercise, drinking, not exerting himself, he ended by scarcely feeling hunger; and by a similar spiritual regime people manage to disguise—for a while—the emptiness of the soul. But, however disguised, that hunger remains.

Under these conditions there is not much future in the effort to *establish our own righteousness*, as St Paul puts it—not much hope of ever being able to turn to God and say, 'Look, I've done all my jobs, so now please give me the pay you promised me.'

So let me silence this stupid and pretentious argument which makes such a noise in my head, this argument which exalts and abases me, and pushes the index of my righteousness up and down the scale; and then perhaps I may hear another voice which says, 'And what about *my* righteousness?—I demand fair trial.' 'But, Lord,' I answer, 'your righteousness is beyond question: who doubts it?' 'Many doubt it,' says the voice; 'they accuse me of hardness of heart. They say I have put man in the wrong and kept him there, that I give him nothing but words to heal his cruel miseries.' 'But Lord,' I may reply, 'I do not accuse you of these things.' 'No,' he says, 'not in words, but I judge you by your deeds. You have a poor opinion of the God who made you, for you do not let me justify myself to you by coming to you, as I desire to do, and living with you, and being your God. How can I justify myself to you, unless you let me do these things? I commended my love to you, in that while you were still in sin, I gave my Son to die for the ungodly; so I sought to justify myself. But I have not justified myself to you, not to you, until you let me treat you as part of my dear Son, and be to you the Father that I am.

'Besides,' says that divine voice, 'I desire to establish my righteousness with others, and not with you only: not here only, but to the ends of the earth. And how shall they hear, and see, and believe that I have given my Son to die and to be their salvation, unless you who are called by his name accept his love and live by his spirit? To establish your righteousness, my child, is a vain endeavour, but I have appointed you to be the means of establishing mine. The task is beyond your strength, and the endeavour to perform it will make ever more hopeless the establishing of your own righteousness; your falling short will be the more evident the greater the things you are called to do. But my righteousness will be the more established: for as you confess your sins it will be seen that I am faithful and just to forgive you your sins, and to cleanse you from all unrighteousness. And even in the matter of your neighbours whom your neglect allows to perish, I will cleanse you from blood-guiltiness, because I am your God, the God of your strength: and so your tongue shall sing of my praise.'

If we should establish our own righteousness, who is the better for it? But if we can establish the righteousness of God, we have secured the foundations of the world and banished all the anxious fears of men. If I could establish my righteousness up till today, it would give me no sure confidence for tomorrow, and beyond the day of my death no confidence at all. But if God establishes his righteousness with us, we are founded on the rock of all being, the will behind and above all happening, the good in whom all evil is redeemed, the life in which the dead rejoice, the sovereign love, unutterable and infinite delight.

Preached at the Feast Service of St Paul's School, an annual service in thanksgiving for the school's founder and benefactors, 28 January 1958. Farrer was an Old Pauline.

Holy Feasts

Wherefore, whosoever shall eat the bread
or drink the cup of the Lord unworthily,
shall be guilty of the body and the blood
of the Lord.   I COR. 11.27

These words appear to us rather gratuitous, and even unkind, when
we hear them in an epistle set to glorify the mercy of the blessed
sacrament; and we wonder what induced St Paul to drag them into
his account of the Last Supper. But if we read his epistle to the
Corinthians straight on, not in liturgical snippets, we see that these
grave words, so far from being dragged in, are the whole point of
what the Apostle has to say. There *was* an 'unworthy eating and
drinking' going on at Corinth—but not at all the sort of thing we
should suppose; it was not, for example, that they came to the
sacrament without repentance, or without devout preparation.
What was going on? Something like this—On what we should call
Saturday evening, but what a person with a biblical background
would more incline to call the eve of Sunday, the Christians of
Corinth collected in Stephanas's house. There was no bell in the
house and there were no clocks in the street: the idea would be to
arrive at sundown, or when you could. Though it was an evening
occasion, the problem of fasting-communion didn't arise in the
modern form; for none of them had eaten anything since a rather
austere lunch or breakfast (call it which you will) and their stom-
achs were as empty as any rigorist could wish. St Paul is writing
about the difficulty of fasting-communion nevertheless; only it
arose for his readers in a different fashion. They all arrived in the
big hall of Stephanas's house at different times, they were all
hungry, and they had all got little packets of provisions in their
hands. For it was to be a genuine communal feast, not only in the
sense that everyone was to come, but that everyone was to contribute to the menu. The rich would bring more and the poor
would bring less, but even the slave could save up a bit of his
bread-ration for the occasion, and contribute something. Then, of
course, they were to share.

To make a fasting-communion under such conditions meant that

you kept your hands off the packet of provisions which lay so
tantalizingly in your own lap until Stephanas, looking in for the
twentieth time, said: 'Well, brethren, I think we are all here at last.
If you will stand, I will make the blessing.' Then taking up a loaf
which had been brought by Crispus or Gaius, or whoever it might
chance, he broke it as the Lord had taught, with prayer, and some
younger men, then or later called deacons, distributed a crumb to
each person present. Having thus broken their fast on the body of
the Lord, they passed their provisions round and ate till they were
satisfied to the accompaniment of cheerful but not unedifying discourse. Then Stephanas collected their attention once more and
blessed the cup.

That was to make a fasting-communion. But the people at
Corinth were not doing this. The early arrivals (presumably the
more leisured and better-to-do) got tired of waiting for the others,
said their own grace and began to eat their own provisions with
their own families or friends. This was supposed to be a mere
snack or *hors d'oeuvre* to keep you going, but it might turn out to be
the substance of the meal, and so when the hungry poor arrived
there was not enough left to relieve their hunger. St Paul (as we
might expect) says it is intolerable. If they really must take snacks
—if, so to speak, they are pampered enough to require bread and
butter or cake at tea-time—then let them have their tea at home and
still bring enough to the Church to share round with their poorer
brethren for supper.

But St Paul does not merely say that such conduct is rude and
unkind and of a sort to disturb the fellowship. He says it is sacrilege. It is here that his modern students are inclined to lose the
thread. Surely not, we say. It may be better to receive the sacrament before other food, but to accuse those who neglect such
advice of taking part with Christ's executioners in tearing his
body, and of eating damnation, is what no Irish village priest,
however rash, has dared to say in defence of fasting. Where, we ask,
is the sacrilege committed? They do not misuse the sacramental
bread, but only the common food before there has been any
consecration—the bread and figs and raisins and nuts in their
packages. How can this be sacrilege?

Well, but to St Paul's mind it is, and to understand him we must
grasp two principles: first, the sacramental bread is blessed as

typical of all their food; and second, the blessing looks backwards as well as forwards. These are hard sayings. Let me explain them.

The sacramental blessing is a Jewish grace-before-meat supernaturalized by Christ. The Jewish form is that we use a single loaf to receive the direct blessing and we give everyone a crumb of that blessed bread; but our purpose is not to bless that loaf and leave the rest unblessed, but through blessing that loaf to bless the meal. And when the blessing receives from Christ a higher power and a higher sense, the same thing remains true—the loaf of the blessing is blessed as body of Christ so that their whole fellowship together through common eating may be blessed as body of Christ. By eating their common supper, so consecrated, they are entering into that mystical union which binds them: they are receiving their common Christendom in bread and wine.

Now to take the second principle we laid down: the blessing looks backwards as well as forwards. When Christ says, 'This is my body,' it is more like the crowning of a hereditary prince than the commissioning of an officer. The prince (in some kingdoms, anyhow) is no monarch until he is crowned. And yet the crowning, at the same time that it makes him king, reveals him as the man who must be king. And when Jesus declares the bread of the fellowship to be his body, he reveals what it is as well as making it what he means it to be. This bread, the bread in which his disciples share their brotherhood—the bread in which they eat the common mercy of God; this bread, summed up and represented in a single loaf, Jesus declares to be his body. If they are a true fellowship of his disciples, and if they are sharing bread and blessing the first loaf in his name—then that one loaf is sacramentally his body, and all their food is the social bond of his body and they who eat *are* his body. Before they eat, when they eat, and after they eat, they are the body of Christ. They eat the body of Christ that Christ may actualize in them what he has given them—their embodied Christendom, their corporate Christhood.

And so we can understand about the sacrilege. Those who divided the bread of the sacred feast before the blessing and ate snacks in corners with their friends, were like those who insult the monarch before he is crowned. For it is indeed the monarch, Jesus Christ, blessed on the throne of his glory, who is blessed in the sacrament of the feast: he reigns in the company of the faithful, he gives himself in bread and wine. When we first hear or read this chapter of 1 Corinthians, we are inclined to say: 'How messy, how irreverent! It must have been awkward, mixing in the holy sacrament with a common meal. I can't think how they managed to switch their religion on and off between the courses.' But when we have reflected a little on the passage, and seen how consistent and how natural it all was, we are inclined to swing right over to the opposite side, and to be appalled not by their messiness but by our conventional piety. 'What', we now say, 'has become of the holy feast? Why is it that religion has been fenced off from cheerful kindness? How has the sacramental principle, intended like the incarnation itself to consecrate the commonplace and join earth with heaven, been perverted into its opposite, and used to make the divine presence something quite apart, locked in a side chapel with a white light before it, put back behind that priestly veil which, by his dying on the cross, Jesus ripped open from top to bottom?'

Perhaps what we need is not an impossible return to first-century customs but the reversal of our own attitude to the customs we have inherited. It is an excellent thing to receive fasting, in the modern sense of the custom, if it helps me to remember that the sacrament is the feast of bread and drink, consecrating all the nourishment that follows it, and especially in its social use, when we eat together. It is less good if the effect of fasting is to make me think that this bread and wine for which I fast have nothing to do with the common nourishment from which I thus distinguish them. It is an excellent thing to kneel before the tabernacle for the wonder of God's condescension—not only, here is God, but, see, he gives himself in flesh, and bread, and takes on common life. It is excellent, indeed vital, that I should bless my ordinary food as well as consecrate the body of Christ, or how shall the two have anything to do with one another? It is excellent that I should often, in my mouth, receive the King of Heaven who died for me, but especially that I should remember how the Jesus whom I eat is the air I breathe, the food on which I live, the common stuff of my daily existence, the society of my friends. All these things are the feast spread for me by hands divine, and all this feast is blessed and consecrated by the blessing of that single loaf, because Jesus died for me and for my friends and for those I do not yet know, but whose fellowship I pray everlastingly to explore in the light of

God's countenance, when I have expiated all my sacrilege in purgatorial fire. Therefore to him who by his death has renovated nature and made common things divine and shone upon our daily path in his epiphany with new immortal light, to him with the Father and the Holy Ghost, One God, be ascribed as is most justly due all might, dominion, majesty and power, henceforth and for ever.

St John's Visionary Epic

PREACHED IN KEBLE COLLEGE CHAPEL OXFORD 1966

A friend of mine, who is a Church historian, heard that I had been writing an exposition of St John's Revelation. 'Dear me,' he said, 'what a very traditional thing to do! There will be a mighty chorus of previous expositors to welcome you into the other world. "So you did one too", they will say. "In that case you will find a great deal to surprise you up here." '

And quite right. The Revelation, in spite of its name, is not a Baedeker's guide to an invisible country, and even if we had made the perfect exposition of St John's text we should still be no nearer to having a map of heaven. For the Revelation is something quite different. And what is it? I propose to dogmatize, because if I put in all the scholarly 'perhapses', I shall not be able to tell you anything in twenty minutes.

Well then: there was a Jewish rabbi in Asia Minor who had probably been crawling about the nursery floor when St Paul preached at Ephesus in the mid-fifties of the first Christian century. After he had completed his studies in Jewish theology he was converted to the Church and, as often happens with converts, there was little love lost between him and the communion he had abandoned. He had the gift of prophecy, as it was then understood. He rose to a position of leadership in the Church at Ephesus and in half-a-dozen cities round about. His name was John.

Whereas the gospel progressed in other centres steadily but slowly, it ran like wildfire in Greek Asia Minor and we know that by the time of Trajan a worried government was trying to repress Christianity in the Province, without more bloodshed than seemed necessary. According to the oldest and best tradition, it was under Trajan's predecessor that John was deported from Ephesus to the Isle of Patmos, but however that may be, it was in the early years of Trajan that he wrote his book, for, in a cryptogram that is not very difficult to read, he tells us so. It was just about the year 100.

It had been John's way to travel round the Asian Churches,

and on the Lord's day to go into the assembly and look the Lord's people in the eyes. Moved by the occasion, he became as one possessed: like an Old Testament prophet. Thus saith the Lord Christ, he declared, and words poured from his lips that he did not reckon his own; flaming denunciations from the mouth of Majesty, and pleadings of divine mercy heartbreakingly sweet.

One Sunday in the solitude of Patmos he felt the pull of his people from the neighbouring coast, and fell under the hand of the Spirit. How should he address the Churches? The Spirit told him —by the pen. There is no reason to suppose that he had ever before done anything so unnatural as to prophesy in writing; but now the occasion and the Spirit constrained him; and he wrote. He spoke to the Churches in writing; and yet, of course, to write is not to speak. The spoken word comes fast, and slips down the wind; the written word comes slowly, and is grown on the page. John meditated deeply as he wrote, and all the Bible came into his mind. He looked with astonishment at what he had written, holy words, words of Christ, and his own page came alive with new visions and fresh voices, pointing him on into the heart of mystery. And so it was that a pastoral letter to seven congregations developed into a visionary epic, condensing the whole tradition of biblical prophecy into a War of Good and Evil, a last battle; the Victory of God, the glories of the World to Come. The movement is ecstatic, the texture is unbelievably close: the inspired author passes forwards and backwards over the unfolding theme, picking up echoes, working up climax, sharpening contrast.

The predicament of the churches St John addresses is absolutely typical. They are terribly weak, exposed to destructive persecution; and yet they are complaisant, rotted by compromise with the heathendom which gapes for their destruction. There are good and faithful Christians in plenty; but they have not (for the most part) the courage of their convictions; they are too amiable to silence or rebuke the deadly propaganda of moral compromise. Such was the Church in St John's eyes. Such is the Church always: I need not tell my hearers that such is the Church now.

St John's message is conveyed by means of a parallel between the little dramas being enacted in the bosoms of the seven congregations and the great drama about to be played out on the stage of heaven and earth. In the Church there is the misleader, Nicolas, the advocate of compromise. St John nicknames him Balaam, after the false prophet of Moses's time who, we remember, sold himself to Balak, an anti-God king. Well, you may not think much of Nicolas, the pocket-Balaam of the seven churches. But look— Satan, defeated by Christ's atonement in the spiritual sphere, turns his mind to politics, and here is his instrument: the false prophet, the enthusiastic minister of a blasphemous worship, the all-out promoter of the Emperor-cult. And here is his Balak, the self-deifying monster to whom he is sold, the last and worst of Emperors, as it were a Nero back from the dead. He has gripped all earthly power in his fist; the nations slavishly adore him; he will push the persecution of the Church to the point of extirpation, and there will be no possibility of resistance. It will be Christ or Antichrist; Christ and martyrdom, or Antichrist and earthly survival. But not for long. The victory of Omnipotence closes the scene. Those who have pierced the Son of God must look him in the eyes: and when they do, they will call upon the rocks to fall on them and the mountains to cover them; they will wish they had never been born.

So St John dealt with Christian compromise by pointing to a future in which no compromise would be possible. The Christians might temporize with Nicolas, the false prophet within their gates; what would they do when the prophet of Antichrist put the pistol of sovereign power to their heads, and said: Your religion or your life?

Well, St John prophesied the end of the world, and it did not come; more immediately, he prophesied Antichrist, and Antichrist didn't come. The end of the world! But the end of the world is always coming: perhaps it is fifty years away from you; at a handsome computation, it is fifteen years away from me. The continuity of history is a mirage. There is no such person as the human race, to drive along that endless road: there is only Tom, Dick, and Harry, and each of them is going slap against the wall. The end of the world is always: it isn't history. No, but Antichrist was supposed to be history; and Antichrist didn't come. All right, he didn't: but it was touch-and-go. The Emperors in due time made their all-out bid to crush the Church; somehow they didn't push it home; and then there was Constantine, and so, here we sit in an Established Church.

St John saw which way the wind was blowing; he could not calculate the exact force of the coming gale. Prediction is the trade of gipsies, not of prophets. A prophet speaks, indeed, of coming time, but it is for the purpose of stripping away false confidence, and showing us where our true assurance lies. Don't let the Christians say that Antichrist will never come. There is no guarantee that he will not; it is the true realism to make your reckoning with the assumption that he will. A Ministry of Defence does not make its calculations on the supposition that the national enemy will never attack. What, then, is the Christians' confidence? Will they, or won't they, put their trust in the love of Christ alone, to save them whether in life or in death? There is only one certain victory, the victory Christ won by dying on the cross, the victory of the martyrs: to conquer is to die.

For the moment, the strife seems terrible, vast, all-absorbing. But patience! How little it appears in the true panorama of heaven and earth! The outbreak of Antichrist is the last convulsive struggle of the old serpent, his head already smashed in by the woman's Seed, the Son of Eve and of Mary. In heaven above a spacious liturgy unfolds, where prayers are incense, angels are ministers, and Christ is the living sacrifice; the face of Fatherhood and Mercy himself is there to heed the world's desire. They pray, he grants: so step by step as the liturgy progresses divine judgement spills over the lip of heaven on the head of earthly evil, and loving-kindness pours on faithful hearts. Even the outbreak of Antichrist is mercy disguised. It sweeps evil into one corner, brigading it under one banner ready for the burning; it gives the martyrs their finest hour, their day of union with the sacrifice and victory of Jesus. It is he who leads them on, and thus they come:

I saw the heavens opened; and behold, a white horse; and he that rode him called Faithful and True; and in righteousness he doth judge and make war: his eyes a flame of fire, and on his head many diadems, with a name inscribed which none knoweth but he himself. He is arrayed in a garment spattered with blood; and his name is called, THE WORD OF GOD. The armies in heaven follow him on white horses, clothed in fine linen, clean white. Out of his mouth proceedeth a sharp sword, wherewith to smite the nations, and he shall rule them with a rod of iron;

he treadeth the wine-press of the fierce indignation of Almighty God. And he hath on his garment and on his thigh a name written, KING OF KINGS AND LORD OF LORDS (Rev. 19. 11-16).

That is the old-world vision; that is the tune to which the martyrs died. Perhaps it is not fitted to our ears, and we may prefer Christ's quiet asseverations, as he ate with his disciples: 'In the world you shall have tribulation; but have a good heart—I have conquered the world.'

Wise Fools

The dean of the royal chapel, Amaziah, priest of Bethel, complains that Amos, a citizen of the sister-kingdom, comes and preaches high treason right under the royal nose, as though an Irishman were to come over and denounce the monarchy in St George's, Windsor. What would the dean say? 'Run away home, you prophet,' says Amaziah, 'and pick up a living in your own country if prophesying can be made to pay there. We don't want any of your impertinence here, and if you aren't gone by tomorrow, you'll regret it, for I've sent a note up to the palace.'

We should like to know whether Amos packed up or not. We are not told, but merely what he said in his own defence. And that is curious enough. 'I am no prophet, nor a member of the guild,' he says, as though that made it any better. Better? Surely it makes it worse. The impertinence is more intolerable if a man who has no professional qualifications or official standing comes and tells us where we get off. If we wouldn't take it from an Irish preacher, is it likely we'd take it from a crofter, raising bad potatoes at the back of nowhere?

Well, but what is Amos's point?—'If I were a professional preacher or politician you might discount me: it would just be what I thought up, in the course of my business, and maybe you reckon you could think up something just as good. But can't you see?— there's nothing in me at all; I might be anyone—I'm just a man to whom a miracle has happened. These words of passion, these visions of clarity, they aren't mine: the Lord said to me, go prophesy thus to my people Israel.'

This is a strange argument, indeed, for what does it amount to?— You must believe God and a fool; you may well hesitate to believe God and a wise man. For with the wise man, how can you know whether it is divine or human wisdom that speaks through him? And human wisdom may be no more than human cunning. Whereas you will easily see that the fool's folly is no part of the wisdom of God.

Fools, children, sinners, these are God's favourite miracles, his chosen evidences; and no one who has met such evidence needs to have it explained, if a poor man with a broken back can be happy by the grace of God; if a stupid child can see, and love, the Universal Spirit whom no man has seen, nor can see, dwelling, as he does, in light unapproachable; if a weak and sinful character becomes the lantern of holiness; if a carpenter with a primary school education is the Son of God, the Saviour of the World.

But if these are God's tokens, is it then a mistake to be sane, healthy, adult, disciplined, instructed, wise? Surely not. How can anything good in itself be a subject of regret? And if God shows his power in giving these gifts to those who have them not, how can it be anything but happy and divine to possess them? We do not have to provide God with bogus children by being childish, or bogus simpletons by being intellectually lazy, or artificial invalids by spoiling a good constitution. For there are plenty of genuine children and simpletons and weaklings and wild men for God's special purposes.

St Paul is able to make the point to his Corinthian converts, that not many wise, not many noble, not many able, were called by God, to make up their new-founded Church; but he can scarcely say of himself, the divine mouthpiece, what Amos said, that he was just a simple chap, for St Paul was about as clever as anyone then alive, and there have been few cleverer since. And, as he says later on in his letter, there is a deep divine wisdom which it is his duty to teach, not to babes, but to those who have the intellectual and spiritual maturity to master it.

Yet, even in his own apostolic work, St Paul feels the pull of simplicity. It may be that he is no plain man, no Amos, and yet, when he first came to Corinth, he says, 'I came with no outstanding display of eloquence or wisdom, I determined to know nothing among you, save Jesus Christ, and him crucified.' He may not be an Amos, but he resolves to behave like an Amos for the while, expunging from his mind all that he knew before, and speaking only of the new calling of God which came to him through Jesus Christ. And why? Because it would be a grievous thing if the Corinthians should come to put their faith in anything human, like the ingenuity of St Paul's theological arguments, and not in the power of God, the God who breaks in upon us all, whether we are simple or wise.

For us who are, or who are at least supposed to be, devoted to the pursuit of knowledge and the cultivation of the intellect, the issue between reasonable enquiry on the one hand, and sheer faith on the other, must always seem particularly sharp. Now I was reading a very persuasive German the other day who had something to say about this which I think St Paul himself would have approved, and which I am now going to try to hand on to you.

What is our perplexity? Is it not that the sphere of science and cool rational wisdom claims to embrace the whole world, and there appears no room left for the sphere of faith? We cannot divide the world between reason and faith, allowing reason to regulate everything beneath the stars, while faith has to do with some infinitely remote world outside the stars, for it is here, in this world, that we meet God, if ever we are to meet him. It is in his potato-patch that the crofter is called to be a prophet and a martyr. So the province of faith, and the province of scientific reason, appear to cover one another completely.

Well, but, says my German, what happened to Amos, when God called him? And what province did God claim as the area in which his creative and redemptive power would move unconfined? The province of open country into which God called Amos, and in which he would transform him from a crofter into a prophet, where was it? It wasn't one part of space rather than another: it wasn't in space, either far or near. No area of space at all, but an area of time—in one word, *the future*. What Amos had been up to that moment was a question of history. A biographer who thought so unimportant a man worth studying, might have reconstructed the whole story from his birth up to that moment from all available evidence; he might have gone back behind his birth into his ancestry. Amos's past, up to that very moment, was all filled and blotted with events, which God himself (now they had once happened) could not change or undo. But the future was a virgin page, the future was open, the future was all God's, and God called Amos forward into it.

God's salvation, from now to eternity, from here to Paradise, is all our future, but the world of scientific enquiry is always the past. No science can study what has not happened: it is only in what has happened that we can read the laws and regularities of nature, and so guess at some general lines which the physical future will observe. But the spiritual future is what we cannot know, and it is into this future that God calls us. 'Forgetting that which is behind, reaching after that which is before, pressing on to the high calling in Christ Jesus'—this is not just youthfulness, or optimism, or the spirit of adventure, it is faith. The past is what I have blotted, I have made it mine, too much mine, by my sins. It is mine, in the sense that I made it so, but not mine, in the sense that I have no power over it; and it throws its grey shadow on the future. Who shall deliver me from the shadow of my past, who shall deliver me from the body of this death? Christ banishes the shadow with his immortal light and calls us into a future which is simply his.

This boundary line between the fixed world which reason studies, and the open world which faith embraces, runs everywhere through the present moment. We are always standing on the brink of the limitless sea, with the neat hedgerows and busy roads carving up the country behind us, and the waves of eternity rippling against our feet; and in our ears the voice calling us of him who walks the waves.

And so, however great is St Paul's wisdom—his knowledge of the historical past, or of the human present—he cannot value it much when he faces eternity: no glances behind, no familiarity with the landsman's map can help him much, when he listens for the voice which is master of the sea.

St Paul was learned, Amos was simple. Amos was a crofter, St Paul was a rabbi. But what called Amos to be a prophet, and St Paul to be an apostle, was neither the simplicity of the one, nor the learning of the other, but that which set a boundary to both— the Word of God, the master of future time. He who studies, studies what God creates; but what God has not yet created, no man can study, only God can reveal. 'Things which eye saw not, and ear heard not, and which entered not into the heart of man, whatsoever things God hath prepared for them that love him: but unto us hath God revealed them, through the Spirit. For who among men knoweth the thoughts of a man, save the spirit of the man, which is in him? Even so the intents of God none knoweth but the Spirit of God. But now we have received no spirit of the world, but the Spirit that proceedeth from God, that we might know the things that are freely bestowed on us by God . . . Who hath known the mind of the Lord, to be his counsellor? But see, we have the mind of Christ'—his mind for our future, for us to walk in love, confidence and light, if we will stretch out the hands of praying faith, and take those things which are freely bestowed on us by God. 'Behold,' he says, 'I make all things new'—and that voice, which shall one day dissolve the world in a flood of light, speaks to us at every moment already: 'If any man is in Christ, he is a new creation: the old things are passed away, behold, they are made new; and all things are of God.'

The Witch of Endor

PREACHED IN THE TEMPLE CHURCH LONDON 1965

There can be little doubt that King Saul's reputation has suffered
unkindly from the propaganda of David and his set. David lived
to tell the tale and he told it his own way. But there were facts
which no propaganda could disguise. Saul was a heroic patriot; he
was the first to break the Philistine yoke; he was the friend of
prophets and a zealot for the God of Israel. And whatever were the
rights and wrongs of the quarrel, David revolted from his liege
lord and proved a thorn in his side. He gathered an army of
ruffians, he took service with the national enemy, and he did not
stir a finger to avert the catastrophe when Saul and Israel fell on
Mount Gilboa by the Philistian sword. The tale of the witch at
Endor is, like everything else, part of the official legend. Saul
goes back on his own salutary laws to traffic in the necromancy he
had forbidden to his subjects on pain of death. And little good it
does him. He has up the ghost of Samuel, the prophet who first
sanctified his throne; and Samuel tells him he is for it.

We do not need to make up our minds about the fact of Saul's
traffic with the witch to recognize that the witch's mediumship is
drawn from the life. No doubt this was the sort of thing that went
on, whether Saul took a hand in it or not. The story is full of
instruction, and so is the biblical writer's attitude to the practices
he describes.

We may wonder what a modern spiritualist is to make of the
story. He may be delighted to recognize that the phenomena of
mediumship have not altered in close on three thousand years.
There is the woman with the special gift of sensitivity; she is asked
to get in touch with a departed person who is named to her; she
uses a technique of some kind to put herself in a receptive state; her
touch with the other world gives her a supernatural knowledge of
personal facts, which is highly impressive to the enquirer. She
immediately penetrates Saul's disguise, and she gives a description
of Samuel which ought not to have impressed Saul as much as it
did—but that also is only panic and too true to life: Saul does not

consider that it scarcely requires supernatural knowledge to describe the dead prophet as an old man wrapped in a mantle. The next stage is that the spirit of Samuel possesses the medium, and answers Saul through her lips. And here too a fact often noted in modern séances appears: the departed spirit speaks pretty much in character. What *would* Samuel have said to a king who by his own admission invoked him because the authorized oracles of God were dumb? He would have said to him, 'You have forfeited the guidance of God by your disobedience; and if God will not help you, then I, who am his mouthpiece, neither must, can, nor will. You can take it you are for it.' And that, of course, is what Samuel *does* say. We need not ask whether Samuel comes to the witch out of the depths of Saul's mind or from her direct acquaintance with Samuel's public image. However that may be, the ghost speaks in character.

So far a modern spiritualist might find encouragement; the phenomena of the cult are timeless, the technique is changelessly effective. But now we reach a more awkward point: the séance is still the same séance, the disclosure of the spirit-world is not the same disclosure. The spirit-controls of the modern medium reveal a hidden world in which a sort of sham-Christian optimism blends with images of material comfort; those who have passed over go on getting spiritually educated in a vague and rather relaxed way; there are spiritual sofas with red plush cushions and tame birds with gold and silver feathers; everything is mildly reassuring and no one ever sees the face of God. How different is the spirit-world from which Samuel speaks! The life of the shades is a deadly sleep from which it is agony to be aroused into mounting consciousness by the pull of the séance. Nothing about it is in the least bit reassuring; there is nothing more terrible that the dead can say to the king, than the words, 'Tomorrow you will be with me.'

If there is one conclusion more obvious than another to be drawn from the comparison of modern spiritist reports with the old Hebrew tale, it is that the séance does not mediate a revelation. The ghost is the mouthpiece of the *Zeitgeist*. Samuel's spirit talks old Semitic pessimism; our modern ghosts underpin a washed-out parody of the Christian hope. If the spirits speak, they tell us what we are attuned to hear.

Now as to the biblical writer's attitude to necromancy. He is bitterly hostile to it and regards it with abhorrence, but he does not take the simple path of denouncing it as a sham. It *seems* as though mediums are able to revive a sort of afterglow of earthly life and he makes no attempt to ridicule the seeming fact. He condemns it in the name of a jealous God. Those who go to mediums are seeking a guiding truth, or an ultimate assurance; why then do they go to ghosts? Why do they not go to God?

Ah, but you may say, that is making it too simple. Where is God to be met with? God is the universal Cause: he cannot act as one particular force, or speak as one particular voice, for God is all. If he teaches us, if he addresses us, it must always be through some part of what he has made. Even if God speaks in my heart, it is by so directing some strand of my thought, as to make it his instrument. And why should not the spirits of the dead be his mouth-pieces?

Why should they not? For half-a-dozen reasons. First, a spirit is dangerously imposing. He is no more than one of God's creatures, and his credentials are dubious, and yet who dares argue with a ghost or doubt his word? As the Hebrew of our lesson shows, a spirit becomes an *elohim*, a God, an authority in his own right, and the heaven of spiritists becomes a republic of ghosts, behind which the living God is veiled.

Second, if God is a living will and a heart of love directly concerned for us, why should we look for him, or why listen for him, in the remote and dubious margins of our experience? It is folly, without a doubt, if we are looking for the evidence of God's creative work, to turn from the living panorama of nature and strain our eyes into the remotest origins of the universe, where we shall descry nothing but the emptiest outlines of astronomical conjecture. And so it is folly, if we seek the master of our life, to look away from the point where God's will touches us in our present existence, into fields where perhaps, perhaps, the sensitive soul makes contact with a limbo beyond the reach or control of reasonable thought.

The lesson of the Old Testament is massively simple—that God and God alone suffices; and that he seeks us where we are, in our present existence, by the voice of prophets who call for our present response, and whose words we can put to the proof by living them out. The lesson is eternally valid; the Old Testament is not annulled by the New. The will of God is everywhere present: it is experienced by being obeyed. When we make our own will the prolongation of God's will for us and in us, then we know God. Saul refuses the Will, the channel is blocked, the oracles are dumb. He goes to the ghosts—and learns nothing to his advantage.

God is here, and we can know him if we will make our account with him: if we will accept his forgiveness for us, and his love for our neighbours, and his plain will for our duty.

'But surely we must look into the spirit world for any hint of a hereafter.' No. What is the ghost's guarantee to us? God is our guarantee. If he will not raise the dead to new life, no power will; for nature will not. The power of the resurrection is God, and God must be encountered here and now. Jesus, putting divine power to the uttermost proof, and dying on the gibbet, can say to the penitent thief, 'Today shalt thou be with me in Paradise.' What a contrast to the word of Samuel to Saul: 'Tomorrow you will be with me.' A later Saul learnt Christ's lesson, and says to us in the Philippians, 'I suffer the loss of all things, that I may gain Christ, and be found in him: that I may know him, and the power of his resurrection, and the fellowship of his passion, if so I may attain to the resurrection of the dead.'

Wishful Thinking

PREACHED IN KEBLE COLLEGE CHAPEL
OXFORD 1962

Do you ever get involved by children in the silly games they play? It's embarrassing. You feel you ought to play properly, or it's a cheat. But there are games like Ludo or noughts and crosses, which you simply cannot lose. There are two or three elementary principles which the poor little beasts cannot master, and which you cannot make yourself ignore. It seems safest to stick to games of pure hazard. But then one has a misgiving: such games aren't very educational, are they?

But worst of all are the games and little rituals which involve wishing. Now I have got three wishes, they tell me, or even one wish, that's bad enough. The child envies me, and can scarcely wait for his turn. He will wish for a real electric model train; she for a doll with real hair, which cries 'Mamma!' when you turn it over. What am I to wish for? They tell me it must be a *real* wish, otherwise I am only pretending. But how do their little minds work? When they do what they call wishing, do they simply throw into words, and say over to themselves, something they wish already? Or must the wish be a new one? If so, how can it be real? I cannot for the life of me produce new wishes on the spur of the moment. Perhaps they can, though; they simply take the lid off their little hearts, and out springs a wish, like a newborn fairy from a magic box. That's what it is to be young.

But I'm wandering from the point: I have still my wish to formulate. I do, of course, wish for various things, but only if they prove compatible with other things. Do I wish that a millionaire, going soft in the head, should read my latest book with unbalanced admiration, leave me his fortune, and die tomorrow? All right, but I ought not to wish for people to die. And do I want him either to be friendless, or to defraud his natural heirs? Do I want the money, if the possession of it will carry all the usual disadvantages which one sees besetting the excessively rich? Suppose I play it safe, and wish that all my wise wishes in the next five years may be granted.

The child won't have that, though, it's a cheat. It isn't *one* wish, I'm overworking the fairies.

But now—oh good!—I remember that Aunt Jane has a headache. I'll wish for poor Aunt Jane's head to clear. I can't go wrong in wishing the removal of a manifest evil. If I'm lucky I'll get away with this. But it is possible I'll be told that the wish must be for myself. Well, never mind, if the game goes on much longer, I'll have a headache, too.

The supposition of the children's game is that wishes made in a certain magic context are self-fulfilling, so long as they are made according to the rules. That is why the adult cannot play the game with sincerity. Who is prepared to endow today's wishes with omnipotence, and let tomorrow be the victim of their inevitable fulfilment?

'To endow today's wishes with omnipotence.' The phrase makes one think: Is not that what we mean to do in our daily prayer? The children's make-believe in fairies is only make-believe, and then the fairies are not supposed omnipotent. Christians do believe in God, and that he is omnipotent, and they put their wishes into his hands. Into his hands, but there is the difference. Into his hands—and he is kind; and so the reasons which make it difficult to wish, do not make it difficult to pray.

All the same, there are similarities. In praying, as in wishing, we are tempted to use blanket-clauses, covering everything, specifying nothing and—of course, in public prayers this is largely inevitable— we express the wish that we may wish for what is good, and that our wishes may be granted. How many of our collects come down to just that. But the collects are common forms, to collect in one the silent and particular wishes of kindred hearts; each one of us must pray particularly. And the same reasons which carried my wishing in the direction of Aunt Jane's headache will incline us to pray with most confidence and simplicity for the removal of manifest evils.

The Bible is full of typical cases of such prayers. Hagar quarrelled with her mistress Sarah (or their children quarrelled, what does it matter?) and Abraham, long-suffering husband, bundled her out into the wilderness with her son. He gave her bread and water; the provision was soon spent, the child fainted. Hagar laid him under a bush and could do no more. She went a few paces, turned her back, and threw herself down. She said, 'Let me not see the death of my son.' What did she want? What was her prayer? Is it necessary to ask? And what do they want, the parents of the starving people to be counted by hundreds and thousands, perhaps by millions—and what would you want if you were there? What would you have wanted if you had passed by where Hagar was? Though, incredible as it may seem, it is possible to harden the heart. So Dives burns in torment, now and everlastingly. For he walked into his banqueting-hall past a starving beggar, horrible with sores.

Yet Christians say that Rogationtide prayers are superstitious. We should pray for spiritual blessings, and leave the great engine of the material creation to grind its inevitable consequences. Yet it is impossible not to pray for bread, when bread is short. The starving cannot be put off with spiritual consolations. Even if they will swallow them themselves, they will not be content to feed them to their children.

Prayer is always possible where wishing is possible, that is, genuine wishing. I hate and fear death, for am not I an animal? Yet I cannot genuinely wish for animal immortality, so that I should sit changeless in my Wardenry for ever. But I can wish, in spite of much sad experience, to increase in virtue. I can wish—there is plenty of scope for the wish—that there may be sufficiency of bread.

When we pray, let wishing take its natural course. First of all, what do I want? Bread for the hungry. Then next, how do I wish, how do I hope it may be assured? My thoughts do not naturally run along Deuteronomic channels. I do not say, 'If only the divine hand would tip (as it were) the great waterpot of heaven our way, we should have first rain then bread.' I do not exclude from my thoughts a divine overruling of natural events—it seems that the physical world has in some respects a looser texture than we had supposed. I can still wish we may be spared floods and droughts. But my hopes and wishes turn more to the direction of human effort when I pray that God may give and preserve to our use the kindly fruits of the earth, so that we may enjoy them: there is still any amount of scope for the improvement of agriculture, and for the fertilization of arid territories, the world over. Why, it would be no fantastic feat to take the salt out of seawater, and pipe it all over the Sahara. It is not harder than flying to the moon; and it is certainly more serviceable. Meanwhile the Sahara is dry.

There is plenty of scope here for us to wish, and where we can wish, we can pray, can present our wishes to the Fatherly Omnipotence of God, knowing that without human wishes he is not pleased to move the mighty mass of men's affairs; but that equally our wishes are dangerous forces unless we submit them to him, and ask for his directive inspiration.

I say that our wishes, un-translated into prayer, are dangerous things. Dangerous things? There is little danger, heaven knows, in those half-wishes, and less than half-wishes, for virtuous objects, which we dutifully serve up in our prayers. What good are they to God, or to us? May God help us to find, and to acknowledge, to liberate and to submit unto his will the fountains of sincere desire which are the life-blood of our mind. This is the evil of Christian hypocrisy: while we are dramatizing ourselves into correct but ineffectual attitudes before God, we cut ourselves off from the springs of genuine will. It was never said of a true saint, you couldn't see what made him tick. Sanctity is the union of heart and brain, submitted to the mind that wields the world, informed by the word of Christ, and aflame with the Holy Ghost.

Loving God and Neighbours

PREACHED IN KEBLE COLLEGE CHAPEL OXFORD 1963

Circumstances have jumped me forward a Sunday, and jumped me out of my proposed subject, and so I ask permission simply to expound the lessons for the day. I take it that you really do want to know what the Spirit says to you through the scriptures, and so, if I expound as faithfully as I can, you won't just think it a bore. Certainly there will be nothing wonderful in a hastily composed exposition, but, if you will let it, the scripture itself will speak; the preacher has merely to keep it before your minds, or, to use less noble language, to rub your noses in it.

To begin, then, with the link between the two lessons. We might fairly describe this as a near miss—for while the scriptures are inspired, the Anglican lectionary, I take it, is not. A *near miss*, because the first lesson, with its supreme claim for the love of God, is directly taken up, *not* in our second lesson, but in the paragraph immediately preceding it in St Luke's text. There it is that Christ draws from the inquiring student of the law a declaration that the law reduces to two articles: the love of God, and the love of our neighbour. Now it is true that the voice of Moses in Deuteronomy does not couple the two loves together as St Luke's student of the laws couples them; and yet the student can claim to be an accurate interpreter, for the book of Deuteronomy taken as a whole is very largely concerned with these two loves. What touching, what intimate directions it gives for neighbourly conduct! If you see your neighbour labouring to raise a fallen beast at the side of the road, you must not pass him by, but lend him a hand; you must not go over your harvest field a second time, but leave the gleanings for the poor.

But we may notice something else in Deuteronomy which appeals to us less. We are to love our neighbours; we are to have no dealings with the heathen, but to extirpate them out of God's own country. Now we Christians are taught to unite the two commands of love: we are to love God in loving our neighbours. He who loves not the brother he hath seen, says St John, how shall he love the God he has not seen? To say 'I love God' and to hate your brother is to show yourself a liar. But in Deuteronomy the connection of brotherly love with love of God is not so evident as the connection between love of God and hatred of idolaters. Love God and him alone; utterly abolish all tokens of rival deities, together with their misguided worshippers.

Now we can see how very sharp and striking is Christ's comment on the Deuteronomic law, which he gives in answer to the young lawyer. Who is my neighbour? The conclusion of Christ's parable is, 'the Samaritan'—the contemporary type of the heretic and foreigner, who pollutes the very air of God's own country, and whom we cannot liquidate as we should, because the even more ungodly Romans won't stand for it.

We observe Christ's method of teaching. If he had been an Oxford ethical philosopher, he would have said: 'In the imperative sentence, "Love your neighbour", your neighbour stands for any man with whom you have to do, even the Samaritan. The sort of thing you must do to fulfil the law, is to lift the wounded Samaritan from the roadside, just as if he were a fellow-Jew.' But Christ does not want to put up logical expositions of neighbourly love, he wants to *make* men love the outcast. And for this purpose it is far more use to show the noble Samaritan in action than to tell a flattering story of a noble Jew. If there is someone you do not like on racial or any other grounds, or if you are temporarily cross with one of your friends, it will do you little good to imagine yourself in the noble act of overlooking this poor chap's imperfections. But if you can recall an example of his unmerited kindness or free generosity, or anything else to warm the heart, then you will just love the man, will you not, and kick yourself for your intolerance or your folly. And still more, if you want to love God, do not make yourself pictures of the excellence or nobility of such an attitude. Just remember who died on the cross, and why he did it. Really there is nothing so useful to a Christian as reading Christ's passion, and meditating on it.

So there is the good Samaritan; he has stolen the Jew's thunder, and loved him first; and how? By picking him off the road and by entertaining him in the inn. We are left with the impression, perhaps, that kindness is the whole duty of man, overriding every other consideration, and that we just can't make too much fuss of our neighbours.

To correct this impression, St Luke takes occasion to give us next the story of Martha and Mary. Martha, like the Samaritan, took in and lodged a traveller: the traveller was Jesus himself. Martha took the view that you can't do too much in the way of material kindness; if only Mary would take a hand, they could do even better. Jesus disagrees. His reply probably contains his usual play of physical symbolism. 'One dish will do. Mary has picked the right plateful, and she shall keep it.'

After all, the cases are dissimilar. The kind Samaritan was saving a life and healing wounds, Martha was just being polite. So far as Christ's physical needs went, one dish would do, and it would be a great pity if hospitable fuss were to prevent Mary from hearing the words of life. For, in a spiritual sense, one dish will do; and it is vital that we should pick the right plateful, and cling to it.

What, in the spiritual sense, is the one thing needful? All sorts of answers have been and still are offered, but in the context of St Luke's story it is really perverse to look any further than the text of Deuteronomy which is his immediate background. 'Hear, O Israel: the Lord, the Lord thy God is *One*, and thou shalt *love* the Lord thy God . . . these words shall be upon thy heart . . . and thou shalt talk of them when thou sittest in thy house . . . and it shall be, that when the Lord thy God shall bring thee . . . into houses full of good things, which thou filledst not . . . and thou shalt eat and be full, beware lest thou forget the Lord thy God . . .'

The one needful dish is the love of God. We shall not get our knife and fork into this dish, says Deuteronomy, if we do not meditate on the words of God; and so Mary had picked the right plateful, when she seized the chance to hear the divine Word, Jesus Christ, speak with his own lips. But all the same, Bible-reading and spiritual discussion are not themselves the one thing needful. Suppose, if you like, that the priest or the Levite going down from Jerusalem to Jericho was so wrapped in devout meditation on the meaning of the Temple-sacrifice he had just celebrated, that he couldn't bring himself to consider the wounded traveller by the roadside. Had he got his knife and fork into the one needful dish? He had not. There are no simple rules about the

form in which the will of God will present itself—at one time a law
to be learnt, at another time a prayer to be said, at another time a
fellow-being to be succoured, at another time a task to be done.
Christ calls on his disciples to be honest, open and flexible in their
attitude to the will of God. For there always is one will for us at
any moment: if we do not embrace it, we frustrate it. To find the
one will of the one God and to do it is our only happiness, and this
it is to love the Lord our God.

The drastically shortened version of the Lord's Prayer, which
next follows in the text, is in its bare simplicity a perfect expression
of the theme, one dish will do. We have been made to think on the
relation between a devout attention to God, and a provision for
physical needs. See then, how St Luke presents the beginning of
the Lord's Prayer: Father, thy name be hallowed, thy kingdom
come; daily provide us with tomorrow's bread. One line for
religion, and one line for bread. He then proceeds: And forgive us
our sins, for even we let off any that owe us debts.

How are we to take this? It is usual with Christian readers to
study St Luke through St Matthew's spectacles, and to suppose
that the meaning is, 'We pray you to forgive us our sins, being (as
we are) ready to let off our debtors: for well we know that the
unforgiving cannot ask forgiveness.' But (to judge by the context
as well as the words) this is not what St Luke means. He is saying
something which sounds on the face of it quite outrageous. 'O God,
be forgiving, for even we can manage that.'

Well, but St Luke cannot really think that Christ meant we
should call upon our heavenly Father to be as good as we are. No,
indeed, the reflexion, 'For even we forgive . . .' is not really
addressed to God, it is an aside we address to our own heart, and,
after all, how much of what we say in prayer consists of such asides!
O God, from whom all good things do come—God does not need
the relative clause, but we need it, so that we may remember that,
in approaching him, we are approaching the source of every
blessing. So, when we ask God for forgiveness, it is vital we should
remember that he really forgives, and to this end we are to recall
the warm compassion with which even a sinful man will let off a
hopeless debtor; and then to remember that God has an infinite
fund of all that goodness which we men have in such short supply.
He really does forgive us, and with all his infinite heart.

St Luke makes his meaning quite plain by going on with parables of Jesus which apply the same point to 'Give us day by day tomorrow's bread.' Give us day by day tomorrow's bread—ah, and you will, for even a bad giver among us would rise from bed and give his neighbour the bread he suddenly needed, if he kept knocking. How much more, then, the fountain of all loving-kindness, the bounty of God! You are our Father, you will do it; for even we sinners are deeply concerned to give good diet to our children.

And then once again comes the symbolical twist. The one dish needful may be a matter of bodily provision, but then again it may not. If ye, then, being evil, know how to give your children good gifts, how much more shall your heavenly Father give—what?—give the *Holy Spirit* to them that ask him. The Holy Ghost is the gift always in season: for he is one with that One Lord whom it is our first and sole duty sovereignly to love; and through the Holy Ghost we shall learn, hour by hour, what is that holy will we should embrace, and through him we shall have grace joyfully to perform it, to the honour of One God in three Persons.

The lessons (Deuteronomy 6 and Luke 10.38–11.13) are those of Easter 5.

Keble and his College

A preacher lately returned from America* may not be expected to bring with him a reverential attitude towards the past. When we tried to give our American hosts an account of our crumbling brickwork, and obsolete heating, their reply was, 'Looks as if you'd better tear it down, and put up something new,'—and as with bricks, so with institutions, and all the shackles of past history. On a commemoration-day, such as this is, we think it decent to put on an attitude of ancestor-worship, and of pious conservatism; just as we put on dress clothes to attend a summer ball. Today we cheer for John Keble, and Dr Pusey, but tomorrow, which of us will want to walk in these men's steps? And why should we? Every generation must solve its own problems in its own way: we cannot adopt the solutions of our predecessors. When they founded the College, they made a forecast of the future, and tailored their proposals to fit it. Their forecast was certainly incorrect, so why should we trouble our heads about their plans?

But are not we tied to them by gratitude? Three thousand persons, mostly of moderate means, subscribed for our residential buildings; only the show-pieces—Chapel, Library and Hall—were paid for by millionaires. The original undergraduates, tied down by rules of bitter austerity, were no doubt encouraged to endure by the thought of all those clergymen's widows, going without marmalade to pay for their rooms. But the widows are now in the enjoyment of everlasting happiness; are, moreover, in the possession of complete enlightenment about the limitations of the Victorian outlook. How can we feel obliged to do what they once thought they wished?

It is certainly important for Christians to remember that they worship a living God, they do not worship the dead. We do not come here to thank our founders, but to thank God for them, and for all the good they did us: and that was certainly a great deal. For here we are, and here we shouldn't be, but for these people's energy and self-sacrifice.

We cannot adopt our predecessors' ideas for us, but we can

* Farrer visited the U.S.A. in 1961, 1964, and 1966.

always learn something from their history. The story of our foundation is a highly creditable one. You may think it was a High Church racket. It was not. It was, above all, a product of the Victorian social conscience. Mid-nineteenth-century Oxford stank of privilege. The general level of expense and way of life among undergraduates was such that the man of moderate means could not study here on a basis of social equality with the rest. As early as 1845 plans were being considered for a more austere, more democratic college, where everyone should have common meals at a fixed charge, and not be allowed to compete in giving continual glorious parties. The excellent Mr Keble, the walking conscience of the Oxford Movement, uttered emphatic approval from his country rectory, and when he died in 1866, the inner ring of those who attended his funeral immediately decided that they could do nothing in memory of him which he would like better than set about building just such a college.

John Keble was born on St Mark's Day, 25 April 1792. On St Mark's Day, 1868, the foundation of the College was laid. On St Mark's Day, 1876, the Chapel was brought into use, and the foundation of the Library and Hall was laid. That is why we keep St Mark's Day, or the Sunday next to it, as our commemoration.

The Foundation was not, as I have said, a High Church racket—and it could not be so, as you will realize if you understand what the principles of those old High Churchmen were. These were not men who wanted to make the Church high (whatever that may be supposed to mean)—they were men who took a high view of the Church. They valued it for what it was, as being divine, and they called upon their fellow-churchmen to exercise their privileges and to honour their inheritance. They could not accept the position of a sect or party without denying everything they stood for. And so, if you look at the records, you will see how emphatically they insisted that all churchmen who cared about being churchmen, should be at home in this College. And to make this clear, they brought in men of official standing outside the Oxford Movement, to sponsor the foundation. It was to belong, not to a party, but to the Church.

Yes, it would have puzzled our founders greatly, to learn that a generation of English High Churchmen would arise, whose most marked characteristic was, that they took a low view of the

English Church, who regarded their membership in it as an accident of birth, only to be tolerated in the hope of seeing it accept
those mediaeval errors which the Reformation had renounced.

Well, times have changed. A paternalism which was taken for
granted in the 1870s would be intolerable now. We no longer force
you to be democratic by forbidding any of you to make your rooms
more comfortable than the College has made them. We no longer
force you into a common pattern of churchmanship by religious
tests or by compulsory worship. We leave it to you to see that no
one in the College is left out, or made to feel inferior, for any cause
—and, after all, *economic* inequality is now probably the least of
such causes. We leave it to you to make such a use of the Chapel,
that the ideal of a common churchmanship on the part of all
churchmen receives genuine and visible expression.

Always, that is, if you approve such aims. For, as I said before,
history is not to bully us; we are to look at it, and to make our
response, in loyalty not to Keble or to Pusey, but to Christ and to
God. Yet we may well reflect that God's good providence has
placed us where we are and so we have a special reason to take note
of our foundation, and see what God wishes us to learn from it.

So let us look for a moment at John Keble himself. No one
knows how many of the pennies subscribed to our buildings were
given in simple gratitude for his personal encouragement, his
gentle advice, or those devout verses of his: verses which enriched
the prayers of a whole generation. What sort of man was it, who
attracted so widespread an admiration? He had certainly done
nothing to court it. Showmanship is the besetting sin of successful
ecclesiastics: Keble had not a trace of it. He published his most
famous book, *The Christian Year*, anonymously and would not
have it mentioned in his presence. He was gentle and unassuming
in his way of talking. His prose writing was plain and unadorned.
He impressed his contemporaries as a saint: it was not only that
he rose so early, and prayed so much, but that he cared so greatly
for God's will to be done, and so little for his own.

We find the seriousness of the nineteenth century oppressive,
and yet, at its best, it was not oppressive at all, but sweet. It is like
the whole-hearted concern of an unselfish lover to please the person
he loves. If a man loves God—how few of us do!—what limits
can be set to the seriousness of his concern? There will be nothing

forced or pharisaical about it; it will be the expression of the heart.

Those who preached at our foundation ceremonies, Wilberforce, Pusey and Liddon, were specially moved to speak of Keble's tender concern for truth. These men had survived into a period when the rise of critical studies was beginning to give to truthfulness, or intellectual integrity, a negative sense. The truthful scholar was to be the man who would not go an inch beyond the support of the evidence. Now Keble had been as scrupulous as he knew how to be in matters of scholarship, but there had been something else in him, which they labour to express. Perhaps they do not do it very well.

I will try to cast a little light on the matter by asking you a question: what is the supreme motive of a truth-seeking mind? Is it to explode shams, or to acknowledge realities? And now suppose that there are realities supremely important, but at the same time too intangible to be proved, will intellectual honesty discount them, or will it embrace them?

It is a commonplace to say, that many things are acceptable to faith, which are not accessible to certain knowledge. This is true as far as it goes—faith is an act or attitude by which we put trust in things unproved by knock-down evidence, but we still want to know the motive on which faith acts. Faith is not its own motive, or ought not to be. We do not want people going about with a sheer appetite for indiscriminate believing. But faith, in the Christian sense, is the twin of love. And love, with its inexhaustible appetite for what deserves loving, sees beyond evidence, sees the soul behind the body, and God behind all. Then faith comes into play—faith, the act of the will, by which we determine to accept, or to worship, or to trust, what draws our love.

But though faith and love go beyond absolute evidence, they are not blind. If we really love and trust another person, we do not wish to entertain a fantastic image of what they are, especially not of their thoughts or desires; and the saint has similarly a fine sensitivity for the revealed mind of God. Such is the truthfulness of John Keble, as his friends had felt it, and as they recalled it after he was dead. He had looked at conscience within, at the situation without, at history and scripture lying behind, with selfless candour, and opened his mind to the teaching of God: for he loved him.

After all the detection of shams, the clarification of argument, and the sifting of evidence—after all criticism, all analysis—a man must make up his mind what there is most worthy of love, and most binding on conduct, in the world of real existence. It is this decision, or this discovery, that is the supreme exercise of a truth-seeking intelligence. John Keble, the gentle, unassuming man, spoke as one who was in contact with this highest truth, for he knew how to stand out of his own light and he had not that strong unconscious motive which shuts our eyes to the will of God—our unwillingness to obey it.

It is right to think that good men who were concerned for the foundation of this College are, in their blessedness, concerned for our continued welfare; that they pray for us, and with us, if we are willing to join them; desiring that we, in our situation, may know the will of God, and do the best for our College, and theirs. In union with them we implore the living truth, the quickening love, the sovereign will, One God in Three Persons, Father, Son, and Holy Ghost.

Moral Perfection not Enough

PREACHED IN PUSEY HOUSE OXFORD 1962

Ye therefore shall be perfect
as your heavenly Father is perfect.
MATT. 5.48

The general idea of this term's sermons is to consider certain substitutes put in the place of service to God, and really a very sensible choice of subject it is. Nothing could be more relevant. For what happens to people like yourselves, people with a Christian upbringing, when they come into this university? It suddenly strikes them, like a revelation, that there is some one thing that really matters, and that this thing isn't religion, whatever it is. There is no great mystery about these revelations, or how they occur. We have always been told that Christianity is caught by infection, or by example, from those who've got it. We come here, and we catch atheism, or humanism, in just the same way. Only that it is not anything so negative as atheism that moves us. It may be political or economic radicalism—when half the world is starving and the whole threatened with military disaster, what can matter compared with rationalizing human justice, and developing human wealth? So to hell with religion. Or it may be something more personal—before I have anything to contribute to mankind, I must stop being the dutiful imitation of my background, and learn to live. Nothing matters, then, but fullness of life. Let me follow my heart, and see that my heart only feels for itself. Or perhaps what strikes me most is the moral quality of the individual. I may not see much prospect that anything I can do will alter the grand pattern of human existence; and as for that other ideal of swallowing one live experience after another, like an *hors d'oeuvre* of oysters, it seems to me a bit greedy. But this is what I would like—I would like to be what I admire. I have a friend who has not a single scrap of religious belief but he's a marvellous person, so cheerful, so brave, so unselfish, so disciplined about work and all that sort of thing; not only can we rely on him, he can rely on himself not to let down his ideal.

At this point (but for Church manners) the Principal and Librarians of Pusey House would leap from their sedilia to interrupt us. 'Come now,' they would say, 'this is absurd. You know quite well that there is no conflict between the service of God and the pursuit of human perfection. Didn't St Alphonsus Liguori say . . .' Thank you, but we don't want to hear what St Alphonsus said. He said a lot and we know that there is a handsome official story about religion improving the character. But that's just what we doubt. It's such a roundabout approach. Surely it's common sense, that if you want to be a good man you should just get on with it. After all, time is limited. There are only seven days in the week. I have fifteen societies to attend, and I can't afford to cut more than 75 per cent of my lectures, and then rowing is practically a whole-time occupation. If I try to keep up with religion on top of all, it will be one more distraction; and then it's all so mysterious and so difficult. If one could *succeed* at religion one might come out smiling and find it a help with being a good man. But how can what one fails at help one with anything? Since there are (apparently) no successes in religion—not even thirds or fourths to be got, but only ploughs—trying to do it only makes one damp, discouraged and morose. It isn't a moral tonic, it's a depressant. Virtue may be difficult, but religion is impossible.

You may think that I'm being ironical and that I don't really sympathize with the point of view I'm stating. But in fact I sympathize with it very much. It is founded on the perfectly sound observation that a great deal of religion is make-believe. The practice of religion can so easily be substituted for real living and real feeling and real thinking. It is easier to keep up a round of religious activities than to be a good man, easier to repeat accepted dogmas than to be mentally alert, easier to perform routine pieties than to answer the claims that humanity makes upon us. True, almost the whole Bible, from the first page to the last, is a protest against the tendency of human cowardice and human sloth to substitute pious mumbo-jumbo of various kinds for a practical obedience to the divine will in the situation which confronts us; and yet,

Bible or no Bible, our cowardice and sloth are still at their old game.

If anyone is ever struck by a true vision of moral reality any-where, let him follow the light. Only, if he will for the moment forget bad Christianity and think of Christ, perhaps he will be able to see that no moral light, however fierce or uncompromising, can lead us away from devotion to the will of God. Christ's sermon on the mountain is uncompromising moralism, yet it is penetrated in every part with the sense of a heavenly Father's will. Do we wish to be the man we admire? Christ says, 'Be ye perfect'—and how?—'as your heavenly Father is perfect.'

Why is not the pursuit of moral perfection enough—or, if that is a stiff sort of phrase, why is it not enough that *I* should aim to be what *I* admire? Why should I need to bring in another party, and another authority, the divine will? Well, but there are two parties anyhow, aren't there? There is the I who does the admiring, and there is the I who tries to catch up with this other 'I', and to be in action what he admires in thought. If you are a moralist, you have a master: a super-ego, say the psychologists; a conscience, say I, because I prefer old jargon to new.

Now the question is simply this: is it more natural to be thus split within yourself, and related to your self, one half pulling and ordering, the other half obeying and getting dragged along; or is it more natural to be one person, united in obedience and devotion to God, related outwards to him, not inwards to half yourself? In my judgement, if you care to hear it, these internal splits, and relations within oneself, are as unnatural as they tend to be tor-menting. As a master to myself, I am so far from adequate. Folly and false directions are some of my troubles, but they are not the worst. Far worse are unforgivingness, discouragingness, and compromise. I cannot forgive myself for betraying myself. Natur-ally not, I am too deeply involved. So I am a terribly discouraging master to myself—until, of course, I can't stand the interior quarrel any more, come down from my high moral horse, and patch up a poor compromise.

If self-government doesn't work, why doesn't it work? Because it's against nature. But what is nature? You may tell me that man is merely an animal that has developed a conscience, and I'm ready to agree. But what's a conscience? It may be no more than a sense for social form, and for what the Joneses expect. But if it is more, then it is a sense for perfection, and the question is, whether my perfection is an idea of mine, or God's will for me. If it is really God's will, and I treat it as my own notion, no wonder I get into confusions and miseries.

The enlightened Christian goes by reason and by conscience, like the enlightened humanist. But for the Christian, 'conscience' isn't my feeling about me, it's God's judgement of me, and 'reason' isn't my power to do moral sums, it's my power to see how the Creator has ordered his creation. The Christian sees back through conscience into God. Conscience isn't a blank wall to him, or a sphinx-like oracle. When the Christian is accused of superstition, for believing in an unnecessary God, he retorts the accusation. No, he says, my hypothesis is rational, and economical: I believe one authoritative will. You think you are atheists, but you are only polytheists; you claim each to be god to yourselves, and carry your private oracles in your hearts. For us there is one heavenly truth, the common light of day, showing all things in their true colours. Only the will that made us can direct us, or show us what we are for.

The divine light shines in unbelieving as well as in believing hearts, but believers have the happiness not to be deceived about its source. Believers see out through the window where unbelievers think that they are looking at a picture flat and opaque upon the wall of a windowless mind. Believers have a blessed relation with a saviour who forgives, instead of an uneasy relation with a remorseful self.

But, of course, the true advantage of looking through the window is seeing what is there. It is always an absurd enquiry, whether it is better to live with God, or without him. The only real question is whether we are without God, or not. Moral perfection itself may be defined as a due response to our environment; and if we have a God—or rather, if God has us—there can be no morality, or honesty of any sort, in pretending that we belong to ourselves.

The supreme Christian comment on the nature of conscience is the Blessed Trinity. Not even the Son of God is God to himself, or engages in moral dialogue with his own heart. And why? Not, heaven knows, because he is morally imperfect, but because he is true to the highest law of being. The loving discourse of the Father and the Son is the very marrow of existence, the very substance of joy. The Christian who embraces the will of God is at one with Jesus, and enters into that divine fire, which warms the heart of the world.

Human and Divine Habitations

PREACHED IN ST BARNABAS OXFORD
AT THE FEAST OF DEDICATION

When I was an undergraduate in Oxford, God began to show me the principles of the Catholic Religion, for I had not been brought up in them. I had a friend of my own age with whom I used to discuss these things, for both our minds were moving in the same direction. One day I said to him, 'This Catholicism of yours, now . . . is it just a theory, or are you going to act upon it?' 'I do act upon it,' he said. 'If you walk in the direction of Walton Street at 10.45 on Sunday morning, you will probably meet me going to St Barnabas's Church,' 'Ah,' I said, knowing that he did not like wordy answers. So, of course, next Sunday I went that way and there he was, walking very fast and straight, as he always did walk, and I did my best to keep up with him, and I came into your Church. The way of worship was new to me, the incense and lights, the music and the silence. And so—for me—I was much moved by it. My friend and I walked away afterwards and said nothing. When we were about half-way home, however, we ventured to exchange a remark or two. We agreed upon a formula. 'There were angels in the roof,' we said. So after that we were always in your church. But, as you see, there are no angels in the roof, that is, no angels carved or painted on the beams. And as to the living angels of God who are present wherever true worship is offered, I do not suppose they have any special preference for roosting in the ceiling. Their wings are all around us, their light is upon us.

Perhaps my friend and I were then about the same age as Jacob, when he ran from Esau's vengeance, and in his destitution and strange loneliness, lying and dreaming at Bethel under the open sky, saw a ladder rising from earth to heaven, and the angels of God ascending and descending upon it. Starting from his sleep, he cried, 'How dreadful is this place! Surely God is here, and I knew it not! This is no other than the house of God, this is the gate of heaven.' Having once found so good a place, Jacob revisited it with tithes and offerings, and so did his children and descendants through many generations. It was their sanctuary, the place of their father's altar, and there they met their father's God.

When the children of Jacob went up to Bethel, what did they go up to see? There was the natural scene, the hillside where Jacob had slept; there were the terraces of rock, rising step above step, which Jacob's dreaming eyes had clothed with angels. But that was not what they went to see, that was not the focus of their devotion, the goal of their pilgrimage. Not all the features of the natural scene touched them so much as that great stone, the biggest he could lift, which Jacob had set there upright on its end, and poured the holy oil upon it, and called it 'the house of God'.

And this is typical of all the holy places of that ancient time. The place where God was to be found was marked always by some dedicated work of man, some venerable stone, some half-broken altar, in which the handiwork of men could be discerned.

But is not this strange, that God should be found in our handiwork rather than in his own; in our little heaps of stones rather than in his mighty mountains? And yet, if we think of it, it is not so strange after all. For what we look for when we look for a shrine, a temple, or an altar, is not simply the presence of our Almighty Creator. What we look for is a place where he is at home with us. When Jacob fled from Esau through strange wildernesses, he did not need to be convinced of God's general power. God's terrible world was all around him in the wind and the rocks and the open glittering sky. What he needed to know, poor man, was that God would come and be at home with him. God in all the great spaces of the world is not sufficiently shown to be our friend. God in the temple which God himself has built is still all his own, he is not yet our God. But if God will accept our welcome, will come and dwell in a temple which our hands, not his, have built, if he will receive gifts from us there and share our hearth; by that act of loving-kindness he shows himself to be our God.

So no sooner had God marked out a place of favour for Jacob, by setting his throne above his dreaming head and sending the angels of his providence down the stairs to him and back again—no sooner had God shown Jacob such a sign, than Jacob hastened to set up a house for God, and pray that he would accept of it, to inhabit there with him. He set up the mere token of a house, a single stone, but it was his work, his building, his dedication, and God's mercy did not disdain it.

If God accepts to dwell in what we have built, then he is ours, he is at home with men; and so men have been always forward to build temples, altars, shrines, that they might have God to be with them. But we notice this about the ancient stories: the temple of our worship was always the place that our great ancestors, Abraham, or Isaac, or Jacob, had built, but at the same time it was a place that God himself had first marked out for us by some special token of his presence. Unless God had appeared to Jacob at Bethel, Jacob would have thought it useless, ungodly, presumptuous, to build an altar there. What right had he to claim that God, the great God, should come down into any stone that Jacob might feel pleased to stand up on end in the open field? But if God himself showed the way, if God came down first and marked the place, then Jacob would build his stones and vow his vow, as called thereto by God's almighty love.

Jacob set up his stone at the point where God's mercy came down to be with man, and his descendants drew the walls of their sacred precinct round that point, so that the single stone became a temple. It is not much different with us. If God came down to Jacob at Bethel, how much more truly did he come down to Mary at Bethlehem. For he came to Jacob in the vision of a dream, he came to Mary in the substance of mortal flesh. If he had not come down to Jacob, Jacob would not have presumed to call God his God, nor make him a house, and if God had not come down to be born and die for us, he would not have been ours, nor should we have been his.

What then? Must Christians go to Bethlehem, to Calvary, to find the footprints of his feet? No, for he has multiplied and spread the place of his appearing. Bethlehem and Calvary are here in every Eucharist, the precious body is stored in every tabernacle. In the midst of every church stands the altar like Jacob's stone—that is the house of God, his body is there—and we draw our walls round it, and arch and roof over it, and so we have our Christian temple.

St John, introducing Christ's incarnation in the beginning of his Gospel, says he became flesh, and *tabernacled* among us. Here God was at home with man indeed, not only dwelling in a human house (for he did that too, at Nazareth) but dwelling in a human skin, flesh of our flesh and bone of our bone. In the same chapter St John goes on to tell us how the flesh of Jesus, like the rocky stairs at Bethel, was marked out by vision as the habitation of God. The vision was shown to John the Baptist, who testified and said: 'I have seen the Spirit descending as a dove and abiding on him. And I had not known him; but the God who sent me to baptize with water, he said to me, on whomsoever thou shalt see the Spirit descending, and abiding, he it is. I testify that this is the Son of God.'

No sooner had he made this proclamation, than two of John's disciples went after Jesus. What was their desire? Their desire was to be at home with the Son of God. 'Rabbi,' they said, 'where abidest thou?' And he said, 'Come and see.' They came and saw where he abode, and they stayed with him that day. There all the quest of God's ancient seekers and worshippers was achieved, when Andrew and his friend stooped their heads to pass under the door of the house where Jesus stayed. Had Jacob, had David and Solomon longed to have God in the house they had built, to be at home with them? The Son of God went into the house of Martha and Mary, to share their table and their company.

Andrew went into Jesus' house, Jesus into Martha's; Jesus' disciples were at home with him, and he with them. 'I in you,' he said, when he sat with his disciples at the supper: 'I in you, and you in me.' Moreover, he gave them this everlasting promise: 'If any man loves me he will keep my sayings and my Father will love him, and we will come and make our abode with him; that is, the Father and the Son will come, for the Son will come, and where the Son is, there the Father is also.'

That is it, then. Here in St Barnabas's Church, in the place that men have built and dedicated, God desires to be at home with you. He is not content to be the God of the world, or to be the God of highest heaven, he must also be your God and inhabit where you have built. Now everything that God desires he desires with the whole of his heart. God has not got a mere corner of his heart for this corner of the world which is called St Barnabas's parish, for that is not what God is like. God's caring for one thing does not get in the way of his caring for another thing: all the world is in his heart, yet he loves every part of it with all his heart. He desires to dwell in every corner and cranny of his creation, and his whole heart is in every such desire. We never have to do with a part of God, with so much of God as God can spare us: we just have to do with God. God is whole, and God is one, and his heart is set on dwelling with you here, and being at home with you here.

You also desire to have him at home with you—but how much less you desire it than he desires it! He desires it with the whole of himself, and how great he is! You do not even desire it with the whole of yourself; no, nor nothing near it. But even if you desired it with the whole of yourself, how little that would be, or rather, not little but nothing, compared with the *All* that is God.

God's presence, spirit, power and love are poured into your church, into your bodies and your souls, like wine into cups, as much as they will contain, and then overflows. All the room you give him, he will fill. And how shall you make him room? How extend his temple? By the faithfulness of your Christian living, by your Christian friendship one to another, your Christian witness to your neighbours, the devotion of your heart's prayer to God. By these things the dwelling of God's mercy shall be extended, though his power fills all extent, and all his works praise him with speechless voices, Father, Son and Holy Ghost; to whom therefore be ascribed as is most justly due all might, dominion, majesty and power, henceforth and for ever.

In Season and Out

Someone has just said to me, 'I hope you saw the effect of the mission in your early Chapel this morning.' 'Yes, certainly,' I replied, 'the congregation was down by a third.' 'Oh,' said my interlocutor, 'that's not the answer I expected.' 'Maybe not,' said I, 'but it was the result that I anticipated.'

I am not repeating this scrap of conversation to show you how clever I am, for it does not take a very brilliant mind to draw the moral from a striking experience half-a-dozen times repeated; and half-a-dozen missions have come and gone, while I have been sitting here.

Why then, in heaven's name, do we have missions? It may well be asked, and the best answer I can give, is that the long-term result is less negative than the immediate effect. But for the moment I am all out to depress you, and it is the immediate effect on which I will turn your eyes.

Perhaps we can get some light on the matter from a parable of Christ, so short, and so bare, that it hardly attracts the reader's attention. A man who had a job of hard work to be done, told his two sons to go and do it. 'With pleasure', said the one, and did nothing about it. 'Hell, no', said the other, or words to that effect, and went and did it. The obvious moral of the story is that deeds are more important than words; but there is a further moral, less obvious—that people have an ineradicable tendency to substitute words for deeds.

Christ's parables are natural stories—they do not need a lot of special assumptions to explain them. That means, in the present case, that we are not to make up a whole novel about the distinct and opposed characters of the two young men, or of how they got to be the way that they were. They are just sons, and we know what sons are like. They have a reluctant regard for the old man, and a certain sense of decency in face of his demands, but then they detest being ordered about, or dropping their own ploys to pick up his. Furthermore, they are brothers, as well as being sons; and that means that whatever line the elder takes, the younger will take the other line. Each has a negative and positive reaction towards his father's wishes, and each gives expression to both reactions. The first expresses loyalty in words, and reluctance in deeds; the second reluctance in words, and loyalty in deeds. They both get everything out of their systems, which is no doubt very satisfactory from the point of view of their emotional health—only one does the job and the other doesn't. The difference may be psychologically trivial, but it has some practical bearing, the father is bound to feel.

The brothers differed in the immediate impact of their father on them. The first was a really nice lad, inclined to smile and say 'Yes'. The idea of pleasing his father was agreeable. The negative wave of reluctance did not rise, until the effort of putting on boots, and getting the hoe, brought home to him what a bore it would be. The other was a horrid boy: his father simply irritated him. The negative wave came straight up, and broke in his father's face. But it had broken, and he went off in full reaction, feeling there was something to be put right and that only one thing would put it right, a spell with the hoe.

Now you think I am all out to scold you, but here is a surprise for you. I do not think you are at all like this horrid youth. When a mission is preached by a great and dedicated man, his words come home with the force of divine love. God speaks, and your reaction to your heavenly father is kind and amiable. You are not at all inclined to say 'Hell, no!'—especially when the spoken word is reinforced by the word clothed in flesh and blood, the living sermon of a Franciscan in our midst, a man who has done what the apostles did, and given up all for the special service of Christ. These things move you, and you take some immediate trouble, perhaps, to interest your friends in what you find holy and good.

Then comes the reaction. We have shot off our religious sentiments. We owe ourselves an amusing Saturday night, and a Sunday morning in bed. It was natural, saying 'Yes' to an Archbishop and a Franciscan: they both had very nice voices. It is equally natural saying 'No' to an alarm-clock: its voice is not agreeable at all, nor is the prospect of slushy snow on the ground outside. We forget that what makes a Franciscan a Franciscan is a habit of getting up at five o'clock no matter what, doing all the menial work that others do for us, and himself looking after what profane lips call the most god-forsaken specimens of the human race.

In the bad old days between the two wars, the capitalist nations endured a boom-and-bust economic rhythm, which was accepted as a kind of fate. It was chastening to reflect, as you went into the boom, that over-production would produce the inevitable slump; and heartening to remember, when several million of your country-men were out of work, that they would not have to starve or idle for more than a year or two, before the compensating boom began slowly to gather momentum. As in *laissez-faire* economics, so in 'go-as-you-please' love affairs, and friendships, too; the boom-and-bust rhythm keeps rocketing to extremes. You think your relationship lies in ruins after the row of last night? Cheer up: *amantium irae amoris integratio est*: 'the falling-out of faithful friends renewing is of love.' You have both worked off your negative emotions in the most satisfactory manner; now is the time for a really juicy recon-ciliation. And perhaps you had better try to forget (since it would spoil the purity of your emotion) that love-feasts produce satiety and renewed confidences lead to further estrangements.

Where people are childish enough, and where their emotional rhythms are in tune, I suppose they may go on like this for a life-time. Quarrelling is a sort of relationship, and anything is better than indifference. Yet they are surely happiest in this kind of life, who live in the moment, and manage not to look before or after. It is better to do this sort of thing, than to know that this sort of thing is what you do.

Especially when the relationship in question is with your Creator, for, to begin with, you cannot get him to play this game with you: his is an unchanging love. Christ is the same today, yesterday and for ever.

Far more serious characters than you or I have confessed a humiliating alternation of moods in their religion:

> Oh, to vex me, contraries meet in one;
> Inconstancy unnaturally hath begot
> A constant habit; that when I would not
> I change in vows, and in devotion.
> As humorous is my contrition
> As my profane Love, and as soon forgot;
> As riddlingly distemper'd, cold and hot,
> As praying, as mute; as infinite, as none.

I durst not view heaven yesterday; and today
In prayers, and flattering speeches I court God:
Tomorrow I quake with true fear of His rod.
So my devout fits come and go away
Like a fantastic Ague: save that here
Those are my best days, when I shake with fear.*

The difference between Dr Donne and us, is that when he was off God, he was frightened of him, and we manage not to be. The same author prays in his *Litany*, 'That we may change to evenness this intermittent aguish Piety'; that is, this recurrent malaria of a religion. And certainly that is the task: not to have booms and slumps, whether over a mission or over anything else, but to go on steadily in a tranquil and loving obedience to God. But how? Perhaps—if I dare suggest to you anything so unromantic—we may get some light on the matter by observing the difference between steady marriages and exciting love-affairs.

The difference to which I will call attention is a difference in the expression of the positive emotion. In love-affairs, it tends to get expressed in common pleasures; in marriage, rather in common enterprises. When the pleasures are over, they are over, and leave the field clear for a reaction. But the common enterprises reach away into the future, and continue to unite us in the pursuit of them. The revolving day brings round its tasks unbidden; common cares mutually endear us, when common delights would only exhaust us.

So, then, the worship of the heart is a fine thing, and it would be wretched if we could never delight in God, or enjoy our religion. But our piety must grow into set customs, continuous enterprises in union with God's grace. If in our worship we can dwell with affection on God's goodness, or in prayer on the names of our fellow men, how excellent. But we must form resolutions. Lord, what wilt thou have me to *do*? What does my neighbour need from me? There is no need for resolutions to be original since we are so bad at keeping them. All we often need is to revive them. What they *must* be, is practical and particular: to pray at the hour I had promised, to be at communion on Sunday, to visit the sick friend, to answer the awkward correspondent, *not* to let so-and-so

* From *Holy Sonnets, xix.*

provoke me, to keep proper hours for my work, to avoid my besetting sin.

And we must examine ourselves when we pray, whether we have done what we promised. It will show us up—but we cannot tell God anything he doesn't know about us, nor, whatever we tell him, is he going to quarrel with us. 'He is faithful and just to forgive us our sins, and to cleanse us from all unrighteousness.'

Jesus

This is going to be a very dry sermon, and indeed hardly a sermon at all. My business is not with pointing morals, but merely with stating facts. I want to say simply that the facts of Christ's earthly life are as solid as a rock.

When some of the papyrus scrolls from the Dead Sea caves were on exhibition in London a secondary school master was trailing a string of young truth-seekers round the sights. 'And there,' he said, waving a casual hand towards the exhibition, 'there are the discoveries which prove that Christianity isn't true.' And why? Because of a tissue of worthless and unsubstantiated conjecture, spun by a professor with a genius for ignoring facts: an ostrich in Penguin's clothing.

A comparison between the Dead Sea Scrolls and the New Testament writings is, in fact, full of interest. Both sets of writings come out of the heart of an established and on-going community. About which of these communities, as going concerns holding a place in history, have we the more and clearer evidence? About the Church, of course: there's no comparison. Again, both sets of writings refer to a community-founder. Which gives us the fuller and more precise information about him? The answer here is even more emphatic: the Dead Sea writings contain little more than hints about that shadowy figure, the Teacher of Righteousness. We don't know his name, we don't know when he lived; perhaps he was martyred—or wasn't he?

The point is more general. We don't know anything worth saying about the founders of any of the Jewish religious sects of Christ's time. Who founded the Pharisaic movement, a movement far more potent and widespread than the Dead Sea sect, whatever that sect may have been? Who was the first Sadducee? Nobody knows. Nobody knows, because the Jewish sects were not interested in their founders, except as men who had laid down rules of life and principles of Bible-exposition. You kept the rules, you went on with the exposition, and you forgot the founder.

The first remarkable fact, then, emerging from the comparison is that the Christians remembered their founder, as a living person, at all. And why did they? Because they did not merely live his teaching, they lived him: they ate him, they drank him, they put him on like the clothes they wore, they talked to him like the friend at their side, they looked to see him face-to-face. All this was new.

Perhaps half-a-dozen years after the end of Christ's earthly life that extraordinary being, St Paul, burst into the Christian movement, and when he'd been at it for some fourteen years he began exploding in letters all over the Greek-speaking world. These letters are inimitably personal and to doubt the genuineness of most of them is ridiculous. Now the modern reader may be disappointed because St Paul does not put anecdotes of Christ's life into his Epistles. Well, he didn't see fit to do it, and that's that. But have you ever gone through the exercise of putting together what St Paul either says or implies about the earthly life and person of Christ? You may be surprised to see what it adds up to. I will anticipate your learned efforts by sketching the thing.

The Jesus of St Paul was Messiah. Was he then a political rebel? Not at all: he was a religious teacher who, like a true rabbi, declared how the divine law-giver was to be obeyed, say in the matter of marriage and divorce. He was also a prophet, who had sketched the shape of things to come. St Paul finds that he and his friends are living out the first part of Christ's predictions, and they look with ardent hope for the fulfilment of the rest. Had Jesus been a miracle-worker? St Paul would scarcely bother to tell us that, since for him the whole life of the Christian movement is lighted up with miracles; that Jesus' own actions should have been non-miraculous, St Paul cannot have believed. What was the nature of Christ's earthly activity? He had been so concerned with preaching the good news of salvation, that he had taken his disciples into partnership and sent them to spread the message, giving them directions about their relations with the people to whom they came: and so, at the time of his death, there was a picked body of his associates in being, called the Twelve. Did Jesus' end overtake him as an unforeseen and unintelligible disaster? No. On the night before he suffered, sitting at table with his disciples, he interpreted his death as their redemption and gave them the symbols of his body and blood to be their food. How came he to die? He died through the persecuting malice of official Jewry, which continued afterwards to pursue his followers; but it was the Roman power that executed him, and by the Roman penalty of the cross. He died, he was buried, and the third day he showed himself alive again, before many witnesses on several occasions, all carefully enumerated by St Paul.

To the historian, the mere bloody-minded historian, the testimony of St Paul is of unique value. He is not an anonymous figure, but a marked man; he does not get his information through a chain of nameless witnesses—he had rubbed shoulders with the surviving companions of Jesus. He could not run off the rails in his account of the tradition about Christ; for he was under the constant check, and sometimes the rival action, of other apostles. The very fact that he makes no attempt to piece Christ's history together frees him from the suspicion of artificial construction. The known truth about Christ simply forces itself into his letters wherever it comes to bear.

And so, as you can see, the gospel-figure of Christ is there, looking over St Paul's shoulder; and the most solid support history can give to the gospel of St Mark is that it bears out St Paul at every point. When did St Mark write? Probably less than ten years after St Paul stopped writing. But this we don't know, nor do we know for sure who St Mark was, when or where he wrote; so we are all the more fortunate to be able to check him by St Paul.

You would not be in the least grateful to me if I were to catalogue for you all the points which St Mark and the other evangelists add to St Paul's outline of Christ's earthly life. But if you are trying to see the general run of events, you may like to observe two crises, or turning-points. First, what fetched Jesus out of his carpentry shop and sent him on mission? Second, why did he go to his death?

The first point is connected by the evangelists with John Baptist. Here was a man calling for repentance in face of a coming Advent of God; and Jesus recognized the authority of his mission and came in with it. But then John was thrown into Herod's dungeon for telling Herod the truth. Then it was that Jesus saw he must step into the firing-line and take John's place. But it was not simply John's place. Jesus had to say, 'There is nothing to wait for: accept the Kingship of God now.' All the other sects of the Jews were keeping the rules of the law, that Israel might be found faithful and worthy when the Divine Majesty appeared. Jesus said,

'The sovereign work of the Divine Majesty is already in action. There is something better than keeping the rules: join in the work, march with the coming kingdom.' And so he told the rich young ruler to sell up and come for an apostle.

And now about the Lord's death. The Jesus of St Mark is spreading the gospel and calling for believers: that is his activity, everything else is incidental. He begins at home, in the heart of Jewish Galilee: he spreads his missions further and further into the foreign communities of northern Jewry. His mission is to the nation and so, when he has preached in Philip's Tetrarchy, he tells his disciples that he can no longer defer an attempt on Jerusalem, the centre of power. And he sees what the outcome will be. Everywhere his preaching has shaken the establishment and frightened authority. He will not get away from Jerusalem alive. But that is no reason why he should desert the souls he came to save. If his life will not do it, his death will do it. He cannot think that the Father, whose loving will he has so intimately explored, will let his purpose fail.

The mission of Jesus was one complex act of love, and of faith; and the gospel preached in his name today is the same gospel that he lived in flesh and blood: 'There is nothing more to wait for. Lay hold of life, it is yours for the taking. The whole saving action of God is in his Son: come with me, share my fellowship.'

The facts about Jesus are just a piece of history. Yet at this point history melts right through: and God is there.

Written on the reverse side of a letter dated 9 January 1967. The allusion in the second paragraph is to John Allegro's Penguin paperback, *The Dead Sea Scrolls*, reprinted in expanded form in 1966.

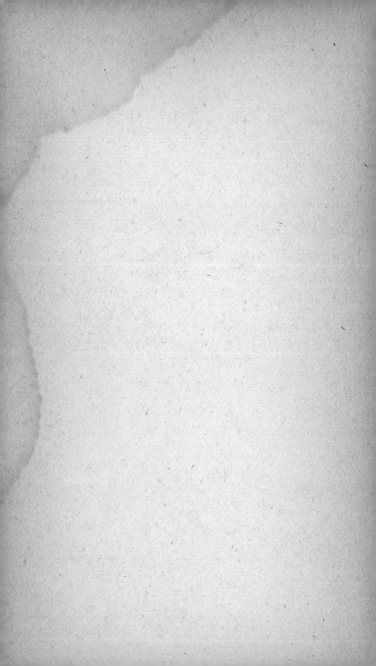

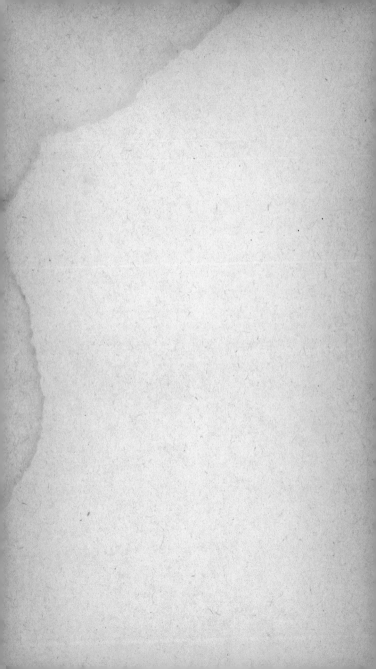